The College Teacher

THE LIBRARY OF EDUCATION

A Project of The Center for Applied Research in Education, Inc.

Categories of Coverage

I	II	III
Curriculum and Teaching	Administration, Organization, and Finance	Psychology for Educators

IV	V	VI
History, Philosophy, and Social Foundations	Professional Skills	Educational Institutions

The College Teacher

HENRY C. HERGE

Rutgers,
The State University

The Center for Applied Research in Education, Inc.
New York

LB
1778
. H4

LIBRARY OF CONGRESS
CATALOG CARD NO.: 66–13407

PRINTED IN THE UNITED STATES OF AMERICA

Foreword

Characteristic of Henry C. Herge is the manner in which he treats the broad scope of material in his monograph THE COLLEGE TEACHER. The subject is dealt with in great breadth. Almost every conceivable concern of the prospective college teacher is touched upon in the text. Helpful observations on such diverse topics as the selection of undergraduate courses, behavioral patterns in the classroom, getting on with one's colleagues, and the role of higher education in preserving a free society are included.

No doubt this is a reflection of the unusual breadth of experience that marks the professional career of Dr. Herge, who has served as teacher and as administrator at virtually all levels of education from the elementary school to the graduate school, at all levels of organization from the local school district to the state department.

Like American education generally, American higher education is marked by great diversity. There are large colleges and small colleges; technical institutes and professional schools; colleges for men and colleges for women; highly selective colleges and colleges admitting virtually any high school graduate; two-year colleges and four-year colleges; colleges in which the intellectual climate is rigorous and those in which the dilettante flourishes; colleges that have abolished intercollegiate football and colleges in which the "autumn madness" seems at times to be their "raison d'etre"— can there possibly be a profession of college teaching in circumstances like these? Dr. Herge shows that the answer is in the affirmative; he describes the characteristics of the profession. However every college teacher must find his own appropriate place in this almost chaotic world. He must be in sympathy with the objectives, program and aims of the institution he serves, or else find another one which he can serve happily. A great advantage of American diversity is that it offers assurance that such an institution in fact exists.

v

Ask a college teacher what he is. He probably will not say that he is a college teacher. More likely he thinks of himself as a historian, a mathematician, or a humanist, and he feels more kinship with colleagues working in the same field in other colleges than with many fellow faculty members at his own college. To emphasize, as this monograph does, the importance of the teaching function in American colleges is not only desirable in itself and helpful to higher education—it is vitally important. But it does not in the least derogate the notion that what a college professor is first and foremost is a man or woman of knowledge. This knowledge he loves, preserves, transmits and enhances.

ALBERT E. MEDER, JR.
Vice Provost and Dean of
Rutgers, The State University

The College Teacher

HENRY C. HERGE

Higher education in the United States currently faces an unusual combination of situations. There are three situations af abundance —students, teachable knowledge, and subjects for research. By contrast, there are three serious shortages—physical plant facilities, supporting funds, and scholars suitable for faculty positions. Of all these situations, the last mentioned is the most distressing. It is with this subject, the college teacher, that Dr. Herge's book deals.

The author treats his subject chiefly from the point of view of the young scholar who is considering a career in higher education, or who has recently been appointed to a teaching position in a college or university. The book furnishes much valuable guidance to such a person. At the same time Dr. Herge has much to say to two other groups already engaged in higher education: (1) members of faculties in graduate schools, who are concerned with the preparation of college teachers; and (2) academic administrative officers in colleges and universities, who recruit and select new members for their faculties, and who provide conditions of service that, hopefully, assist beginners to develop into the sort of mature and competent teacher-scholars that are the pride of every worthwhile institution of higher education.

Dr. Herge reviews the current programs for the preparation of college teachers and finds much need for improvement. Here and there over the country he finds evidence of a developing sensitivity to the need for a truly professional program for preparing college teachers in the graduate school. He focuses attention particularly on the desirability of a supervised internship experience in college teaching for the graduate student, before he is awarded the Ph.D. and turned loose on hapless undergraduate students as an assistant professor.

Although Dr. Herge's book is directed mainly to members of the academic community, it is rich in the sort of information that should be of interest to any citizen who wishes to be well informed about the current situation in higher education in the United States.

JOHN DALE RUSSELL
Content Editor

Contents

CHAPTER I

Higher Education in American Society

Currently there are an estimated half million educators serving in American institutions of higher education as teachers, researchers, and administrators.[1] This professional staff, already of impressive size, will grow still larger in the foreseeable future. College and university faculty members collectively carry a tremendous responsibility; their task is the proper education of the young men and women who, on reaching maturity, are most likely to become the leaders of thought and action in the United States and, to no small extent, in many other countries throughout the world. Broadly stated, those who instruct at the college level are expected to guide and assist students toward maturity along two somewhat different lines: (1) in specific character development; and (2) in the acquisition of intellectual skills and new concepts of knowledge.

The primary task of the American college teacher is to provide a cultural environment for students, offering a variety of intellectual experiences which hopefully will enable them to fulfill their obligations as free agents in a democratic society. The teacher hopes to achieve his goals through consistently planned activities for students, designed to kindle within each the spirit of creativity and inquiry, to foster the habit of making objective appraisals and choices, to develop the stamina of emotional discipline, and to cultivate conscience and strength of will. The college teacher places high value on student educative experiences calling for the organizing, initiating, and directing of mental activity with the confident expectation that these experimental exercises will promote desirable changes and elicit increasingly mature human behavior. Effective teaching thus requires a remarkable aptitude for bringing all these activities into close harmony in order to produce responsible

---

[1] *Summary Report, Faculty and Other Professional Staff in Institutions of Higher Education, 1963–64*, U.S. Department of Health, Education, and Welfare, Office of Education, OE–53014–64 (Washington: U.S. Government Printing Office, 1964).

1

citizens in society—citizens with enough strength of character to render their own objective judgments.

To assist students in acquiring knowledge is a second, and secondary, task of the college teacher. This objective characterizes all levels of the educational system, but the transmission of knowledge is especially critical at the college level where, hopefully, youthful concepts may be refined before becoming the commitments of maturity. The enormous expansion of knowledge achieved in very recent decades has provided a greatly expanded content of information that must be acquired by on-coming generations. The chief burden of passing on the higher levels of this new knowledge tends to fall on teachers at the college and university levels. As more and more young people are being educated over longer and longer periods, the emphasis in collegiate instructional programs is tending to shift strongly toward this secondary objective of imparting knowledge. Though much time and energy are used up in expanding facilities, improving quality, refining entrance requirements, strengthening standards for student retention, revising curriculums, and gearing programs for technological eras, all these are essentially a part of the secondary, rather than of the primary task.

Among college teachers, the fainthearted, the intellectually mediocre, the menial followers, and those lacking vision, dedication, or love of liberty, will be content to achieve only the information-giving objective. First-rate minds, however, can be expected to keep clearly in view the primary importance of preparing students for effective membership in a democratic society. Acquisition of knowledge is essential not primarily for the sake of the knowledge itself, but for the manner in which sound knowledge affords the basis for effective rational processes.

Today's world requires that educational institutions be positive and compelling forces for the preservation of freedom, as well as agencies for producing the highly skilled professional manpower needed in a dynamic, scientifically oriented society. The nation now faces a crucial period in its development. Its life and the lives of its citizens depend on the effect education has on college students—on their acceptance of the ideals of freedom, and on the extent to which they manifest the desire to preserve their heritage. One may ask specifically, will the students' intellectual experiences equip them to reason well for themselves? Will those who have had the advantage of higher education accept their responsibility as full members of society by participating constructively and conscientiously in all areas of human relationships?

The type of person recruited to college teaching is of critical importance, for it is the college teacher who determines whether or not the power of education will invigorate democracy. If colleges and universities fail to attract and retain faculty members who are scholars equipped to discharge effectively their function as teachers, then indeed the very survival of the nation will be in serious jeopardy.

The Challenge of Change

Recent decades have brought marked changes in the economic, social, and political situation in the United States. As most Americans are aware of these changes, there is no need to describe them extensively here. However, few should be mentioned because of their impact on higher education and on the responsibilities of those who teach in colleges and universities.

Rapid growth in technology has resulted in a greatly increased national productivity which has raised the level of personal income allowing more opportunity for leisure. This growth has provided challenges as well as comforts, with its need for technicians capable of carrying on and improving the productive processes. By the end of World War II the United States rose to a position of international leadership which made heavy demands on the country's resources and trained manpower. After the war, the nation's intense concern about defense distorted the interest of budget makers and legislative appropriating agencies. This led to a heavy concentration of support for scientific and technological fields, and to a corresponding neglect of the humanities, the arts, and the social sciences. The spread of Russian communistic ideology among some Americans, and the success of the Russians in launching their first Sputnik, led to a searching criticism of the entire American educational system. As a result, educators were blamed for having failed to prepare the citizenry for such developments.

The roots of many of these social, economic, and political changes extend back much farther than the decade of the 1940s. During the twentieth century the economy of the United States has changed from rural-agrarian to urban-industrial. Consequently, middle-class parents began to recognize that education was the "open sesame" for their children—the key for entering the professions and for increased opportunities for the entire family.

Each year the demand for trained manpower in our highly technological economy requires that more and more young people pursue their education beyond high school. The rising level of family income has made it financially possible for a larger and larger percentage of the on-coming generation to be supported through the years of college attendance. No longer is the labor of all young people in the college-age group needed to maintain the economy. Current predictions suggest that more than two-thirds of the children born since 1943 will enter college, whereas only one-sixth of the United States population now over 54 years of age have attended college, and less than one-half of these have earned degrees.[2]

The College Teacher in the Contemporary Scene

New frontiers in the curriculum. In one lifetime American higher education has moved abruptly from its traditional curriculum, centered in the liberal arts, to a proliferation of undergraduate and graduate curriculums geared to a broadly functional theory of education. This transition has been neither smooth nor uniform. Because of the decentralized, pluralistic nature of the system of higher education in the United States, there have been wide swings to extremes with marked differences between and among individual institutions. Educators and institutions may be found which staunchly defend almost any philosophical position one could cite, from curriculums that are functional, vocationally-oriented, or student-elected, to a single, mandated, uniform curriculum for all students.

In their concern for defining and fulfilling their emerging functions, college and university professors have been analyzing the purposes and content of their course offerings in relation to their students. As a result of this assessment, college teachers have

---

[2] Harvey E. Brazer and Martin David, "Social and Economic Determinants of the Demand for Education," in *Economics of Higher Education*, Selma J. Mushkin (ed.), U.S. Department of Health, Education, and Welfare, Office of Education, Bulletin 1962, No. 5, OE–50027 (Washington: U.S. Government Printing Office, 1962), Chapt. 2.

brought their instruction into line with changing social needs. At no time in educational history have so many new curriculums, courses, and textbooks been developed, nor have so many challenging innovations in instructional methods and materials been introduced before in college classrooms, giving new form, depth, and direction to modern teaching.

In the twentieth century, college teachers not only have to prepare undergraduate and graduate students of high ability in the professional fields, but also have to train students in specialized, highly technical fields, most of which are of national concern and importance. Outside the classroom, college professors serve in remote and unexpected settings in a never ending quest for new knowledge. In institutional libraries and laboratories, university and college teachers have become increasingly involved in the spirit of pure inquiry. Scientific, technical, and social developments in the United States bear witness to the efforts of college teachers.

Academic circles are not in agreement concerning the professional mission of the college teacher. One group argues that the role of the true scholar is limited to the pursuit of new ideas, to experimental thinking, and to independent research and discovery. Another argues that the teacher-scholar must be concerned with instructional effectiveness in the classroom and lecture hall, with research for curriculum development, and with leadership in learned societies. A third group, influenced by the "land-grant college" philosophy of service, maintains that the legitimate concerns of scholars in a changing society must be research on practical, everyday problems, advice to communities struggling to improve their services to their citizens, and programs of education and technical assistance for newly developing countries throughout the world—all conceivably consistent with the basic purposes of the college or university! These three points of view may be found in varying combinations and strengths on almost any campus.

Nearly every college and university has experienced the rising demands by students and faculty members for new and expanded curriculums. Before a faculty can adopt a more functional curriculum design it must clarify its fundamental purpose. Few colleges have been financially able to implement fully their professional judgments in these areas. Most colleges have had to make compromises under the stricture of inadequate budgets.

Institutions' efforts to compensate for financial inadequacies are varied and almost uniformly unsatisfactory in their effects. Fund-raising becomes the all-consuming pursuit of presidents. Facilities, equipment, and materials are replaced only as they reach total obsolescence. Choices have to be made between appointing fewer faculty members, altering the pupil-teacher ratio, or offering minimal salaries. New programs are viewed critically if they are likely to be costly. The net effect of these and other economies is that the poorly financed institution engages in a mere holding operation, and inevitably loses ground as it fails to go forward with its more generously supported fellow-institutions.

Nevertheless, one can be optimistic as American colleges and universities today face a crucial test of their ability to anticipate and fulfill the needs of a dynamic, changing culture, for an outstanding characteristic of the American college or university is its remarkable ability to adjust, to expand, to be highly flexible, even to be compound, and yet to retain its basic functions in contemporary society.

The public image of the college teacher.   In the past the public image of the college and university teacher has been unfavorable. Fictional stereotypes, as seen in newspaper cartoons, motion pictures, and recent novels portray the professor as an absent-minded nitwit, totally out of touch with the practical world, centering his attention on a small area of perfectly useless knowledge. He has often been caricatured as a wild-eyed lunatic, wearing a disarranged academic gown and mortarboard. Belok[3] reported a disproportionate number of abnormal characteristics in both men and women college teachers in the novels of the 1940–57 period. The cumulative effect of the fictional stereotype has been negative. The popular notions endure that classroom teaching and academic life are inevitably drab and boring to any normal person, and that the cloistered existence wears upon beginning college teachers until they eventually succumb to dull and monotonous conformity.

In contrast with the view of the college teacher held in the past by the general public, the image of the professor presently held by students tends to be somewhat more realistic and favorable.

---

[3] Michael V. Belok, "The College Professor in the Novel, 1940–57," unpublished doctor's dissertation, University of Southern California, Los Angeles, 1958.

Some recent studies,[4] made to determine student evaluations of fifteen different occupations normally attractive to college graduates, show that undergraduate men students rate college teaching first in a cluster of four high-level occupations, in this order: college professor, lawyer, doctor, and business executive. When the finalists in the 1963 National Honor Society Scholarship Contest were announced, these superior high school seniors, for the sixth consecutive year, listed teaching as the profession they would most like to enter. The only career choice that interested more boy finalists than teaching was science, while among the girls science stood second to teaching.[5]

Deliberate effort has been made in recent years to supplant the widespread negative image of the college teacher with a more realistic picture. Television has been of considerable help. In 1960 a television program entitled "Meet the Professor" was initiated on the recommendation of the Association for Higher Education through its Committee on Teaching. The purposes of the program were: (1) to show the college professor as a stimulator and exemplifier of inquiry and creativity; (2) to develop interest in college teaching as a career; and (3) to show the college teacher as a vital and contemporary person, both in his work and in other aspects of his life. The successful achievement of these goals has been attributed to the high quality of the series, which received an award for distinguished interpretation of higher education in 1962. In this, and in current TV programs as well, the college teacher is no longer commonly cast in the unfavorable image of the dilet-

---

[4] For a comprehensive treatment of the student's image of the college teacher and of factors influencing the choice of college teaching as a career, see:

College Student Images of a Selected Group of Professions and Occupations, Final Report, Cooperative Research Project No. 562, U.S. Office of Education (Middletown, Connecticut: Wesleyan University Press, 1960).

John E. Stecklein and Ruth E. Eckert, *An Exploratory Study of Factors Influencing the Choice of College Teaching as a Career,* Final Report, Cooperative Research Project, U.S. Office of Education (Minneapolis: University of Minnesota Press, 1958).

R. E. Welch, Jr., "What's the Image?" in R. O. Bowen, ed., *The New Professors* (New York: Holt, Rinehart & Winston, Inc., 1960).

Donald D. O'Dowd and David C. Beardslee, "The Image of the College Professor," AAUP *Bulletin,* XLVII, No. 3 (September 1961), 216–21.

[5] National Education Association, *The Future Teacher* (Washington: National Commission on Teacher Education, NEA, Fall, 1963), Vol. IX, No. 1, p.1.

tante, the snob, and the ineffectual egghead. In the eyes of the public he is becoming the erudite gentleman on the panel show, the astute lecturer on "Sunrise Semester," the economics professor who advises the President on fiscal matters, the Nobel Prize winner who perfected streptomycin, the scientist who produced "heavy water" for the Manhattan Project, the Assistant to the President of the United States for Science and Technology.

Public images affect the destiny of individuals, organizations, and nations. As the image of the college professor improves, and college teaching thereby gains status, the recruitment and retention of top caliber men and women will be less and less difficult. At present, progress toward increasing the number of effective college teachers promises to be good. If the trend continues, one of the long-term problems in American higher education will be solved.

Intellectual and personal factors.   College and university officials consistently seek to recruit faculty members from among the intellectually gifted—from the extreme upper part of the continuum of the normal distribution of human intelligence. The professions, industry, and government are also bidding for the services of the relatively limited supply of people with this high level of intellectual ability. The maintenance of salaries that are attractive in comparison with those offered in other occupations is essential for successfully recruiting faculty members for institutions of higher education. In addition to the competition for high level talent within the business world, there is also keen competition among institutions of higher education to lure the nationally recognized scholars who also have an interest in teaching and research for faculty membership. The success of an individual college or university in attracting these highly capable faculty members depends largely on its willingness and ability to match the salaries and other conditions of service that prevail in the relatively few prestige institutions.

For the young person who would like to become a college faculty member, intellectual excellence is a quality of prime importance. Intellectual excellence, like professional respect, is not given —it is earned. Through independent study and research, the modern college teacher tries to maintain an awareness of the frontiers of human knowledge, tries to keep abreast of developments in his specialized field, and tries to be responsive to the demands of research and of teaching at the same time. Constant application is required if he is to achieve professional recognition both as a researcher and as a teacher of college students.

While scholarship is a highly important quality in a good college teacher, other characteristics are also of great importance. Certain personality traits tend to be associated with superior intellectual endowment. Among these are: (1) social and emotional adaptability; (2) curiosity, interest, and enthusiasm for information concerning man and his environment; (3) commitment to self-defined values; (4) physical and intellectual energy to expend in pursuit of professional interests; (5) facility in critical analysis; (6) the sense of proportion that permits humor; and (7) creativity.

Probably the most telling indicator of a college teacher's professional promise is creativity, that rare personal quality that seems to characterize all great teachers. In recent years interesting experiments have shown that teachers may stimulate their own as well as their students' creative functioning. It has been demonstrated that creative thinking among students flourishes best within settings that are informal and permissive; but creativity seems to disappear rapidly whenever the learning environment is strained or the situation demands conformity. The creative intellect cannot be contained by the status-quo. It often infects both students and faculty colleagues by reason of its sheer enthusiasm. Soon an entire class or a whole campus can become infected with new ideas and exciting learning possibilities.

Regardless of how unusual a teacher's intellectual qualities and temperament are, if he is not imbued with the excitement of learning and is not possessed by a passion to communicate his discipline to others, he is not fit to teach. He who labors as a college teacher has an abiding mission: he must transmit knowledge and skill in which he is proficient to the succeeding generation, but, even more important, he must assist the members of that generation in developing the intellectual virtues that are essential if they are to fulfill their obligations in a democratic society. Since superior intellects are needed in the sciences, medicine, industry, and government, one ought to demand that those who educate these intellects be at least as intelligent, knowledgeable, and skillful as their products are to be.

But what of the young, untried candidate for a college teaching position? Evidence from which institutional officials try to estimate an applicant's potential intellectual excellence is not entirely lacking. The fact that a candidate has earned an advanced degree in itself indicates at least minimal intellectual ability. The quality of the program at the institution from which he received the degree is another indicator. Comments by those who have been his instructors are useful, though what is not said about a former student is sometimes more significant than what is said. His academic transcript will indicate the quality of his performance as a student and the breadth and depth of his experience in the various subject matter fields.

Probably nothing contributes more, in the long run, to the creation of a truly great college or university than wisdom exercised in the appointment of new faculty members.

The Academic Marketplace

Measures of the demand for college teachers. The most baffling problem facing American higher education today is preparing a sufficient number of qualified personnel to meet the constantly expanding need for faculty members. The current critical shortage of college teachers developed in part due to the gradual decline in the birth rate during the 1930's, when it reached an all-time low. Then, quite abruptly, came a reversal of the trend. In the early 1940's, especially after the close of World War II, the birth rate rose and has continued at a high level to the present. The relatively few born during the period of low birth rate in the late 1920's and 1930's provided a meager supply of young adults in the late 1950's and the 1960's from which new college teachers could be recruited. This insufficient supply of teachers came at a time when the colleges were filled, if not overcrowded, with students born since the early 1940's, during the period of higher birth rates.

Another factor affecting college enrollments, besides the midcentury of population growth, is the heightened interest of young people in attending institutions of higher education. In 1900 only 4 per cent of those in the 18–21 year age-group, a mere 230,000 students, attended college. In 1961 the 18–21 year age-group numbered more than 10 million and almost 40 per cent were enrolled for degree credit in colleges and universities. This college age-group is expected to number 14.6 million by 1970, and 16.3 million by 1975, when according to the Bureau of the Census there will be approximately twice as many in the college age-group as there were in 1957. Other forecasters freely predict that more than 50 per cent of these 18–21 year olds will be attending college.[6]

Enrollment statistics over the past 20 or 25 years reveal the meteoric rise in the number of young men and women going to college. In the autumn of 1964, the total enrollment of full-time, part-time, and extension college students was a little more than 5.3 million; in 1950 the figure was about 2.7 million; it was about 1.5 million in 1940.

The number of students seeking admission to college is expected to double in the decade of the 1960's, and progressive increases will be registered between 1970 and 1980. To compound the problem, actual enrollments have consistently surpassed all earlier long-range projections, suggesting that the estimates for 1970 and 1980 may be conservative. Changing conditions, including unpredictable demographic, political, and socio-economic factors, will doubtless affect the demand for college-educated people. But whether enrollment projections prove to be ultra-conservative or exaggerated, the demand for college and university attendance cannot be met at a quality level unless prompt and drastic measures are instituted to provide an adequate supply of well qualified instructors.

With a projected enrollment for 1970 of about 7 million, of which at least 4.5 million will be full-time students, the required number of new college teachers will average about 31,000 per year. If modern teaching techniques, such as television and programmed learning, are not widely used, this number will be necessary annually to meet the projected expansion in enrollment and to make up for normal replacement of those retiring for various reasons.[7] Another study by the U.S. Office of Education estimated that each year in the decade 1960–61 through 1969–70 about 36,000 new college teachers would need to be prepared at the master's and doctor's degree levels and to be retained in service

---

[6] Louis H. Conger, Jr., "College and University Enrollment: Projections," in *Economics of Higher Education*, Chapter 1.

[7] "Ten-Year Objectives in Higher Education Staffing 1960–1961 Through 1969–70," *Higher Education*, XVII (February–March 1961), 3–14.

in order to replace those retiring and to staff the expanding enrollments.[8]

The qualification ideally sought in employing new faculty members is the doctor's degree, but the annual production of doctorates in the United States did not reach 10,000 until 1960–61, and even now is not far above that figure. It must be remembered also that probably not many more than half of those receiving doctorates go into college and university teaching; thus the current supply of fully qualified persons is grossly inadequate to meet the demands expected in the years ahead.

A report[9] issued in the spring of 1963 contrasts the markedly improved situation in the preparation of new public school teachers with the decline in the quality of the preparation of new college teachers:

> In this decade which marks the greatest advance in the preparation of public-school teachers, both elementary and secondary, the institutions of higher education were losing ground. Between 1954 and 1959 the per cent of new teachers entering full-time college service as holders of the doctor's degree declined from 31.4 to 23.8, and in 1963 it stood at 25.4. Over the 10-year span those with one year of training beyond the master's degree increased slightly, from 18.2 to 20.3 per cent, but new teachers with just the master's degree increased from 32.2 to 39.4 per cent. The necessity for accepting many new teachers with obviously insufficient training is shown by the fact that in 1954, 18.2 per cent of the new group had not yet attained master's degree status. This figure went as high as 23.1 in 1957 but declined to 14.9 in 1963.

The ratio of the supply of competent scholars to the demand for their services in colleges and universities varies widely from one subject matter field to another. A recent report[10] confirms the as-

---

[8] U.S. Department of Health, Education, and Welfare, *Ten-Year Objectives in Education: Higher Education Staffing and Physical Facilities, 1960–61 Through 1969–70*, prepared by the Office of Education at the Request of Secretary of Health, Education, and Welfare (Washington: Office of Education, 1961), p. 3.

[9] National Education Association, Research Division, "Need for College Teachers Grows," *Research Bulletin*, XLI (December 1963), 109. For full details see biennial study.

———, *Teacher Supply and Demand in Universities, Colleges, and Junior Colleges, 1961–62 and 1962–63*, Higher Education Series, Research Report 1963–R3 (Washington: National Education Association, May 1963), pp. 9–31.

[10] Kenneth A. Simon, *Instructional Staff in Institutions of Higher Education, Projected to 1970–71*, U.S. Department of Health, Education, and Welfare, Office of Education, Circular 715, OE–53018 (Washington: U.S. Government Printing Office, 1963).

sumption of some appointing authorities that shortages in the principal fields of instruction will continue, if not worsen, in the years immediately ahead. The study also provides the hope that staffing conditions in time may improve; but, since education is a slow process, especially at the graduate level, several more years will be required before enough college teachers, well qualified with doctorates, can be produced to relieve the acute shortages in most of the subject fields.

Economic status.   Academic circles have long recognized that faculty salaries were too low. Institutions have been under great financial pressure, and increases in support have barely kept pace with the insistent demands for expansion of facilities. The demands for expansion have been along two fronts: first, to provide instruction to the rapidly increasing number of young people who want to attend college; and second, to extend the curriculum by providing instruction in the new fields of knowledge that have been opened by the research of scholars. It is to the great credit of American colleges and universities that they have, in general, managed their resources so that nearly all qualified young people have been able to matriculate. Curriculum expansion has also been prodigious. Both of these developments have required the addition of large numbers of new faculty members. Thus, increases in available supporting funds have been used by most institutions primarily to employ more faculty members; improvement in the salaries of existing staffs had to be made only with resources left over after meeting the urgent demands for additional instructors.

Particularly since the end of World War II, the salaries of college teachers have lost ground in terms of buying power compared with other professions and occupations. Ostroff in *The American College*[11] quotes Beardsley Ruml showing that between 1939 and 1957 real income (that is, with the purchasing power of the dollar accounted for) had increased 79 per cent for all forms of employment in the United States; but faculty salaries, in terms of real income, had actually decreased 8.5 per cent, whereas average income of doctors and lawyers had risen sharply. Ostroff further described the resultant economic pressures upon college professors, noting

11 Anthony Ostroff, "Economic Pressure and the Professor," in *The American College: A Psychological and Social Interpretation of the Higher Learning,* Nevitt Sanford (ed.) (New York: John Wiley & Sons, Inc., 1962), pp. 445–62.

that the equivalent salary of a professor receiving $7,000 in 1904 should have been about $35,000 in 1957. As a result of their low academic salaries, professors have been harassed by professional and economic woes, including: (1) debts; (2) family problems arising from inability to support dependents properly; (3) necessity for extra employment, which restricted time for preparation, research, reflection, relaxation, and informal association with students; (4) curtailment of social relationships outside academic circles, which often led to a closed social, psychological, and political experience; and (5) emotional problems arising from feelings of guilt, insecurity, and frustration.

In the mid-1950's the economic status of the profession began to improve. In 1955, the Ford Foundation's College Grants Program offered financial incentives to about 100 accredited privately-controlled institutions that had made realistic approaches toward upgrading their salary schedules. Later the plan was broadened to include 630 colleges and universities that qualified for Foundation grants for endowment specifically restricted to faculty salary improvement. Other agencies followed suit, and publicly controlled institutions were able to use these examples of improved support to influence larger appropriations from legislatures for faculty salary increases.

In 1957 the President's Committee on Education Beyond the High School published the shocking conclusion that college teachers were in effect subsidizing the education of their students by an amount more than double the total of all gifts and endowment earnings combined.[12] The goal proposed by the President's Committee was doubling the average faculty salary in a ten-year period ending in 1967–68. Though great strides have been made toward this goal, the gap that remains is a cause of disappointment in academic circles. The initial impact of the Committee's announcement seemed to be effective in inducing a flow of gifts and grants from corporations and individuals, as well as in gaining improved treatment of higher education by legislative appropriating agencies; but the rate of salary increase has not been sufficient to create real optimism.

Actually faculty salaries had been on an upward trend for a few

---

[12] President's Committee on Education Beyond the High School, *Second Report to the President* (Washington: Government Printing Office, July 1957), p. 4.

years prior to the report of the President's Commission. The average salary increased 6 per cent between 1954 and 1955, and also 6 per cent between 1955 and 1956; there was a 9 per cent increase between 1956 and 1957. The percentage increases for 1959–60, 1960–61, 1961–62, and 1962–63 were, respectively, 6.9, 5.7, 6.5, and 5.8. The trend has been under study by the American Association of University Professors in its annual survey of faculty salary scales.[13] In most years the average rise in faculty salaries has been considerably below the 7.4 per cent increase needed to reach the goals of the President's Committee before the end of the decade.[14]

The American Association of University Professors, with headquarters in Washington, D.C., has been active and influential in promoting the upward trend in faculty salaries. This association some years ago began the publication of an annual rating scale by which colleges and universities are evaluated on the basis of the average and the minimum salary for each academic rank. Colleges and universities are graded from AA, the highest (which only a few attain), down to F, the lowest on the rating scale (which is still above the salary levels at a number of colleges). The salary levels required for the attainment of each rating are revised upward annually, in accordance with the general trend for improvement of faculty salaries. Those institutions which permit the Association to publish their faculty salary data are listed in an annual report, so that the general levels of their faculty salaries for each

---

[13] "The Economic Status of the Profession, 1962–63," AAUP *Bulletin,* XLIX No. 2 (June 1963), 141–42.

[14] Detailed data on faculty salaries in American colleges and universities are available in a number of sources:

Louis A. D'Amico, *Higher Education Salaries 1963–64,* U.S. Department of Health, Education, and Welfare, Office of Education, Circular 759, OE–53015–64 (Washington: U.S. Government Printing Office, 1965).

Ford Foundation, *The Pay of Professors.* A Report on the Foundation Grants for College-Teacher Salaries (New York: The Foundation, February 1962).

"The Economic Status of the Profession, 1962–63: Report on the Self-Grading Compensation Survey," AAUP *Bulletin,* XLIX, No. 2 (June 1963), 141–87.

The economic status of the academic profession for the selected years 1939–40 to 1964–5 and projected salary trends for 1969–70 are reported on in the AAUP *Bulletin,* LI, No. 2, June issue, 1965.

National Education Association, Research Division, *Salaries Paid and Salary Practices in Universities, Colleges, and Junior Colleges, 1961–62,* Higher Education Series, Research Report 1962–R3 (Washington: National Education Association, February 1962). Attention is called also to the biennial survey for 1963–64, listed in footnote 15.

academic rank can readily be observed. The Association also projects ahead for several years its salary standards for each academic rank and each grade on the rating scale, so that institutions, in making salary adjustments for a coming year, will know approximately where they will be rated. The tabulation shown herewith indicates the projections of the scales for the various ranks and grades for 1964–65 and for 1968–69.

TABLE I

Standard Scales of Average and Minimum Compensation
Projected for 1964-65

Average Compensation Scale

	AA	A	B	C	D	E	F
Professor	$22,110	$17,840	$14,310	$11,880	$9,770	$8,020	$6,890
Assoc. Professor	14,110	12,110	10,470	9,000	7,840	6,830	6,020
Assist. Professor	10,460	9,120	8,080	7,120	6,400	5,770	5,240
Instructor	7,860	6,840	6,200	5,650	5,270	4,930	4,640

Minimum Compensation Scale

	AA	A	B	C	D	E	F
Professor	$16,260	$13,790	$11,490	$9,820	$8,360	$7,070	$6,150
Assoc. Professor	11,730	10,210	8,940	7,790	6,850	6,030	5,340
Assist. Professor	8,900	7,830	6,970	6,180	5,550	5,030	4,590
Instructor	6,790	5,960	5,430	4,950	4,630	4,340	4,080

Standard Scales of Average and Minimum Compensation
Projected for 1968-69

Average Compensation Scale

	AA	A	B	C	D	E	F
Professor	$27,000	$21,500	$17,000	$13,600	$10,900	$9,000	$8,000
Assoc. Professor	15,500	13,500	11,900	10,400	9,000	7,900	7,200
Assist. Professor	12,000	10,700	9,560	8,580	7,760	7,100	6,600
Instructor	9,000	8,300	7,680	7,140	6,680	6,300	6,000

Minimum Compensation Scale

	AA	A	B	C	D	E	F
Professor	$18,500	$15,500	$12,900	$10,750	$9,050	$7,800	$7,000
Assoc. Professor	13,500	11,700	10,100	8,750	7,650	6,800	6,200
Assisst. Professor	10,000	8,900	7,940	7,120	6,440	5,900	5,500
Instructor	7,500	6,950	6,470	6,040	5,650	5,300	5,000

Source: AAUP *Bulletin* Vol. L, No. 1 (March, 1964), p. 35.

The customary practice in American colleges and universities is to assign faculty members academic ranks indicative of their scholarly maturity. A beginning teacher with minimal preparation is normally assigned the rank of "instructor." As his preparation and experience progress satisfactorily, the instructor may expect to be promoted to "assistant professor," then to "associate professor," and finally to the highest academic rank, "professor." In some institutions the designation "distinguished service professor" is accorded a very few outstanding faculty members. In the analysis of faculty salaries it is useful to note the averages and ranges for the various academic ranks, for these figures tell something of the progress in earnings that a young instructor may look forward to if his services are considered fully satisfactory.

Biennially the National Education Association compiles data on salaries paid instructional and administrative personnel in each academic rank for all classifications of colleges and universities in the United States.[15] Figures for the academic year 1963–64 show that median salaries for full-time teachers for the nine-month academic year ranged from $6,114 for instructors to $7,539 for assistant professors, $8,969 for associate professors, and $11,312 for professors.

Median salary figures (the figure at which half the salaries are above and half are below), as cited above, give an incomplete picture of the wide range of salaries currently being paid instructional personnel in colleges and universities in different teaching fields, in different academic ranks, in different kinds of institutions of higher education, and in different geographic areas of the nation. For example, the National Education Association report referred to above showed 119 full-time professors in the New England region with salaries of $20,000 and over for nine months of service in 1963–64. In that year the median salary for a total of 9,506 professors in the same geographic region was $12,429.

All ten of the recent biennial surveys of faculty salaries by the National Education Association indicate that college faculty salaries have moved upward consistently. These raises, however, were smaller and came later than the salary increases in the same period for those with comparable preparation and experience serving as professional and administrative personnel in business and industry. For more than two decades the colleges lost many promising teachers to the professional labor market, where the lure of good sal-

---

[15] National Education Association, Research Division, *Salaries Paid and Salary Practices in Universities, Colleges, and Junior Colleges, 1963–64,* Higher Education Series, Research Report, 1962–R3 (Washington: National Education Association, February 1964), p. 5.

aries is a significant factor in attracting and retaining personnel of high intellectual quality. This competition continues to plague higher education generally, though it is much less a matter of concern in the few high-prestige institutions where the academic market place has become a "seller's market," especially for top-flight scholars and researchers who can practically set their own terms of employment.

The majority of teachers in American colleges and universities come from the lower-middle or upper-lower socio-economic classes. They find the profession more "socio" than "economic" in its advantages. Only for those of the lower classes have the financial rewards of college teaching proved significantly greater than those offered in their fathers' occupations. For those of upper-middle class backgrounds, the remuneration for college teaching suffers sadly by such a comparison. Consequently it takes considerable motivation and enthusiasm for teaching (and possibly a private income) to entice students from wealthy families into college teaching careers, though some are attracted because of a profound respect for the scholarly life and atmosphere.

One of the features of college teaching that is often attractive to young people from the middle and lower class homes is the possibility of vertical social mobility—the opportunity to move into a group of higher classification socially. Those from lower class backgrounds who are not particularly acquisitive may be enormously satisfied with the intrinsic pleasure and status afforded by membership in a community of scholars. Unfortunately, many of the really talented beginners soon decide that they cannot maintain their new found status on their income as beginning college teachers, and other professions, eager for their services, offer substantial financial inducements. Improved salary conditions, however, are currently encouraging the best talent to consider seriously careers in teaching.

Teaching opportunities for women.   According to a report by the U.S Office of Education, women comprised 22 per cent of the teaching force in institutions of higher education in the United States in 1961–62. In 1909–10 the percentage was 20.1; it increased until it was 27.6 per cent in 1939–40. Then the percentage of women began to decrease, standing at 23.5 in 1951–52. Small but steady decreases have been shown in each biennial survey since that date.[16] The low ratio of women to men teachers in higher education persists despite the avowed readiness of college and university appointing authorities to employ more women. Inasmuch as the population contains about as many women of high intellectual capacity as men, the possibility of increasing the supply of capable faculty members by attracting more women into college teaching seems worthy of exploration.

The low percentage of women among those who earn doctor's degrees partly explains why relatively few women are college teachers. The report of *Earned Degrees Conferred 1961–62,* issued by the U.S. Office of Education[17] shows that of a total of 11,622 doctor's degrees conferred that year, only 1,245, or 10.7 per cent, were granted to women. In that same year, however, women received 37.7 of all bachelor's degrees granted, and 30.8 per cent of all master's degrees. The proportion of doctor's degrees awarded to women had hovered around the 10 per cent mark each year for the preceding decade, and indeed the percentage has been low ever since American universities first began to grant the Ph.D. degree.

If the number and proportion of earned doctorates conferred on women is to increase markedly, the universities will have to establish challenging and accessible programs for young women who may be ideally suited for careers in college teaching. At present this reservoir of teaching talent is largely monopolized by the elementary and secondary levels of education in the United States.

Public school teaching and nursing, traditionally the most acceptable professions for women, have often been more "processional" than "professional" for the women who enter them. Interruption for marriage has meant a high annual rate of replacement. The average young woman in America is married in her late teens, before she has had opportunity to qualify for a bachelor's degree. Her family of two or three children is completed and half grown by the time she is in her thirties. No longer bound to household

---

16 Ralph E. Dunham and Patricia S. Wright, *Faculty and Other Professional Staff in Institutions of Higher Education, First Term 1961–62,* U.S. Department of Health, Education, and Welfare, Office of Education, Circular No. 747, OE–53000–62 (Washington: U.S. Government Printing Office, 1963).

17 Wayne E. Tolliver, *Earned Degrees Conferred 1961–62,* U.S. Department of Health, Education, and Welfare, Office of Education, Circular No. 719, OE–54013–62 (Washington: U.S. Government Printing Office, 1963).

chores in an era of automation and "instant everything," she is ready to search for new and challenging employment.

Since the early 1950's, the demand for technically and professionally trained personnel has provided both single and married women more abundant and varied employment opportunities than ever before. Those married women who have the essential preparation usually return to their previous occupations. Those without it enroll on a part-time basis for preparation for a wide variety of occupations. With continuing domestic responsibilities, they often prefer to enroll in college and university courses on a part-time basis, and in an institution within easy commuting distance from their homes. By this means married women who had not completed preparation for some profession before marriage may take the courses required to qualify for a useful field of service, such as teaching. Those who had three or four years of undergraduate study before marriage may undertake a program of advanced study, possibly leading to the master's degree, and may thus qualify with minimal preparation for college teaching. Those with high intellectual abilities can be encouraged to proceed toward the doctor's degree, though university requirements usually specify at least one academic year of full-time study in residence for the doctorate. However, a number of universities, particularly those located in urban centers where there is some concentration of married women who desire further education, now cater to this clientele by adjusting schedules and instructional programs for their benefit.

The idea of attracting increasing numbers of women to college teaching is entirely feasible. Those already in service are performing creditably. The rapidly growing junior colleges are finding an expanding source of much needed teachers among the highly capable women who have completed requirements for the master's degree. Many have reached this level of academic attainment after marriage, or after some experience in elementary or high school teaching.

The creation of a pool of talented women interested in college teaching has been suggested. This might lead to the establishment of a national roster of specialized female talent for the use of college and university officials in recruiting faculty members.

CHAPTER II

The Modern College Teacher

Modern curriculum patterns and techniques of teaching in American higher education reflect the concepts and practices of an academic society that flourished in Western Europe for some centuries before the establishment of the first colleges in Colonial America. These concepts and practices, having become traditional, have promoted uniformity in higher education through subsequent ages and continue to influence strongly the policies of American educational institutions.[1]

Following the European tradition, college teachers in the early days of American higher education were not expected to be specialists in any particular subject. Each member of a college faculty could and often did teach any and all subjects in the limited, fixed curriculum. In Colonial times, and in fact until well toward the end of the Nineteenth Century, most American colleges were small by modern standards. Often there were no more than four, and sometimes fewer, faculty members. One professor might teach all the subjects taken by freshmen; another the sophomore subjects; a third the junior subjects; and a fourth the senior subjects. For the most part, the college professors of that day had no earned degree higher than the bachelor's. They gained the advanced scholarly attainment that made them eligible for faculty membership by wide reading, by writing and lecturing, and not uncommonly by a period of service in one of the learned professions, particularly the ministry.

During the latter part of the Nineteenth Century two forces combined to necessitate the present practice of each college teacher being a specialist in one, often relatively narrow, field of instruction. The first of these forces was the expansion of the curriculum to include many subjects that had not been taught formerly at the

---

[1] For a treatment of the historical perspective, see Hugh S. Brown and Lewis B. Mayhew, *American Higher Education* (New York: The Center for Applied Research in Higher Education, Inc., 1965).

college level. The second was the rise of German scholarship and the introduction in the German universities of advanced degrees that required the candidate to concentrate his advanced study in some small segment of an academic discipline. American universities in the last quarter of the Nineteenth Century began to develop graduate schools modelled on the German pattern, and their requirements for the graduate degrees, particularly the Doctor of Philosophy, closely followed those of the German universities.

Early in the Twentieth Century educators began to express concern, both in this country and abroad, about the quality of American higher education. In the United States the Federal Government did not (and still does not) exercise any control over the quality of institutions of higher education, in marked contrast with the practice of the governments of many European countries. Voluntary agencies known as accrediting associations were formed to certify the quality of colleges and universities in the United States. These accrediting agencies have set up standards which an institution must meet before it can become a member and thus be "accredited." The early standards were based arbitrarily on the judgment of the best scholars of the time. In the 1930's research was undertaken which placed the accrediting procedures on a sounder basis, so that each criterion could be shown to have a demonstrable relationship with institutional quality.

From the inception of the accrediting movement, the standards emphasized the preparation of the faculty as an index of institutional excellence. The measure most commonly used was the number of faculty members holding the doctor's degree. The research done in the 1930's on the accrediting procedures thoroughly substantiated this measure, and to this day the number or percentage of faculty members holding advanced degrees is about the only measure of faculty preparation commonly used in evaluating institutions of higher education. It is almost axiomatic today that "the higher the percentage of faculty members holding the Ph.D., the better the institution."

It should be noted that the Ph.D. degree, as developed originally in Germany and as copied faithfully in the graduate schools of the United States, is essentially a preparation for a career in research. The candidate must have mastered a subject matter field, which may be relatively narrow, but this is conceived mainly as a basis for his research. The most critical requirement for the Ph.D. degree is the production of a dissertation representing a "contribution to knowledge" based on the candidate's own original investigation. None of the usual requirements of a university graduate school for the Ph.D. degree directly prepares the candidate for teaching at the undergraduate level, other than the experience he has had in going through that same subject matter himself, probably at a time somewhat remote from the completion of the doctor's degree. Usually the doctor's candidate is required to pass some kind of a preliminary examination on the field in which he is specializing, but this is not generally viewed as a test of mastery for the purpose of teaching that material. Probably the fledgling Ph.D. retains some impressions of the methods used by his own instructors in undergraduate classes—impressions often formed prior to his own commitment to a college teaching career, and therefore probably neither critically observed nor accurately recalled.

In general faculty members in American colleges, from Colonial days to the present, have been "culled" from the annual supply of college graduates rather than prepared for their instructional roles. Even after there began to be insistence on graduate degrees, the advanced studies offered in graduate schools were not directed primarily toward preparing college teachers. The graduate school still tends to look on college teaching as a by-product rather than as its chief objective. Historically the prime requisites for college teaching have been few: (1) a scholarly mind; (2) a desire to teach at the college level; and (3) an earned degree. As noted earlier, since the last decade of the Nineteenth Century there has been a growing insistence that the degree be at least the master's and preferably the doctor's. A respectable concentration of studies at an advanced level in the subject to be taught is also expected.

Notably absent in the list of requirements is any evidence of professional preparation or demonstrable competence as a classroom teacher. A candidate for a college teaching position rarely is asked to present proof of satisfactory completion of a supervised internship in college teaching under professional direction, and, if such a requirement were made, few indeed could meet it.

For centuries college teaching has been teacher-centered. The instructor's classroom is a sacred precinct, not to be violated by supervision by a college officer who might be interested in seeing how effective the instructor actually is in his classroom performance. Thus the college teacher has been free to rely on traditional classroom procedures. He has tested his success as a teacher by his students' ability to master facts and subject content, as demonstrated by their performance on examinations he has constructed. Rarely has he been expected to show how his facts, skills, ideas, value judgments, and insights were transmitted and reinforced. Methodology has been the concern of no one but the practitioner himself. Consequently his instructional procedures have consisted mostly of little but lecturing, assigning required reading, and giving oral and written tests on information which the students have learned largely by rote.

The old requirements for college teaching have changed but little up to the present. As previously noted, a graduate degree, preferably the doctor's, is almost essential. Willingness to teach, to do research, and to write is the second criterion. Despite all the publicity about the critical shortage of effective college teachers, few universities have maintained well formulated programs designed to recruit and prepare college teachers. Emphasis in graduate schools is still on the preparation of researchers, skilled in techniques of investigation, concentrating on a narrow field that will be of value to them as productive research scholars. In filling positions on college faculties, most institutions still hopefully cull the annual lists of those prepared for careers in research, or proselyte their needed talent from other campuses, or wait expectantly in line (behind industry and government) to greet the yearly crop of graduate school products.

During the past two or three decades many college teachers have become increasingly aware of the need for examining the process of learning and the methods by which classroom effectiveness might be improved. As a result, the demand for pre-service and in-service programs for training college teachers appears to be growing. For three or four decades groups of college presidents have been urging graduate schools to provide preparation directed toward the specific needs of the prospective college teacher. The typical response of the graduate school deans has been to "pass the buck" back to the undergraduate colleges; if only, they say, the colleges would give thorough training to those coming fresh with bachelor's degrees to the graduate schools, the problem of effective college teachers would be solved. The result has been a stalemate. Furthermore, the same college presidents who resolve that graduate schools should do a better job of preparing college teachers seldom express a desire to obtain someone with professional preparation for college teaching when they approach a university appointment office for suggestions of candidates to fill a vacancy. Understandably, then, the graduate schools have not moved in the direction of providing this kind of training. From their point of view, any relaxation of the rigorous requirements for the Ph.D. degree would be a debasement of the academic currency, and to add new requirements of professional preparation would lengthen the candidate's educational program inordinately, and possibly to no very good purpose.

Here and there, reports indicate that small programs have been organized specifically for the preparation of college teachers. These have usually been within a single department, or a small group of departments, in the graduate school of a university. From these beginnings it is hoped that a widespread program of professional preparation for college teachers may be developed eventually. Such a program should improve instruction at the level of higher education as much as the corresponding movement during the first half of the Twentieth Century has improved teaching at the elementary and secondary levels of the public school system.

Traits of an Effective Teacher

Whatever else he may be, however renowned in his field of specialization, no matter what his acclaim as lecturer, author, or researcher, the faculty member becomes a *teacher*—nothing else—when he stands before a class of students.

Judging from the literature about the really "great teachers" one would conclude there is no common mold for effectiveness. Though "great teachers" have forceful personality traits, their biographies reveal no common pattern of academic interests, outward physical appearances, rapport with students, classroom climate, or philosophy of education. The portrayals of these "great teachers" reflect only in a limited degree the modern-day students' idealized formulations of the qualities most esteemed in their college professors.[2] In fact, history is replete with dramatic examples of teachers of acknowledged distinction, who exhibited some patterns of class-room behavior that would not be admired widely today. Some of these "great teachers" were men of rare intellectual ability and at-tainment whose idiosyncratic behaviors frequently eclipsed their social skills and organizational abilities.[3]

Basic inherited tendencies. The old cliché may still be heard in academic circles that the few truly great teachers—the ones who achieve the applause of their students—are the born teachers. Few educators will deny that certain inherited propensities prob-ably contribute to a teacher's effectiveness in the classroom. At the same time it is unreasonable to assume that success in teaching can be guaranteed if potential candidates are screened primarily with reference to the possession of favorable basic inherited tendencies. Admittedly, new systems of prediction have been designed to esti-mate a candidate's probability of success in teaching. The criteria of potential effectiveness in these systems are, by and large, ob-servable behavior characteristics usually associated with success. The various measuring instruments focus attention upon such char-acteristics as: (1) contagious enthusiasm for one's field of teach-ing; (2) ability to verbalize and communicate easily with individ-uals and with large groups; and (3) sympathetic interest in the individual problems of students. These studies indicate the need for further research primarily to determine the extent to which measuring instruments specific to the various types of instruction are necessary and then to validate the findings.

Because teacher performance is one of the most complex of human phenomena, and because the teacher shortage is becoming more serious each year, it would be a dangerous mistake to com-plicate the task of staffing the nation's colleges and universities by relying solely upon predictive instruments yet to be fully validated.[4]

---

[2] Robert H. Knapp, "Changing Functions of the College Professor," in *The American College,* pp. 303–307.

[3] Houston Peterson (ed.), *Great Teachers: Portrayed by Those Who Studied Under Them* (New Brunswick: Rutgers University Press, 1946), p. 347.

[4] For comprehensive reports on recent research on teacher behavior and assess-ments of teacher effectiveness see:

David G. Ryans, *Characteristics of Teachers: Their Description, Comparison, and Appraisal* (Washington: American Council on Education, 1960).

Paul L. Dressel and Associates, *Evaluation in Higher Education* (Boston: Houghton Mifflin Company, 1961).

The time has come for the college teacher to recognize that knowledge of one's discipline and possession of certain basic, inherited tendencies are not sufficient to insure success in imparting knowledge. Though the favorite theme, "Teachers are born, not made," creates a dichotomy between teaching skill and knowledge of subject matter on many campuses, a revival of interest in effective instruction is taking place. Respected leaders in higher education are advocating that all potential teachers have some practical experiences in supervised teaching as part of their preparation programs, as well as courses or seminars in the theory of learning and in the functions of the college teacher:

> What is needed is a revival of the art of teaching in colleges, for it is a fallacy to expect that the ability to teach in a college is a miraculous gift automatically bestowed as a bonus with the Ph.D. degree and which is, by some magical process, at the demand of every college appointee, without effort on the part of the recipients.[5]

Personality characteristics. Teachers vary widely in their personal attributes and classroom behaviors. In the past, lists of salient personality characteristics of successful teachers have been promulgated by institutions for teacher preparation. Usually these lists were so all-inclusive that the reader was led to believe that only a divine being could embody so many good qualities.

Recent studies signify, however, that the desirable intellectual and personal characteristics of a teacher are not absolutes. An important study of this difficult and complicated area, dealing with ". . . identifying certain types of teacher traits that are significantly

---

M. Vere DeVault, Dan Anderson, Dorothy Swain, and Patricia Cautley, "Teacher Education and the Study of Teacher Classroom Behavior," in *Theory Into Practice,* Frederick R. Cyphert (ed.), Vol. III, No. 1 (February 1964), 21–25.

J. M. Stephens, "Traits of Successful Teachers: Men or Angels?" in *Theory Into Practice,* Philip W. Jackson (ed.), Vol. II, No. 2 (April 1963), 59–66.

Kenneth G. Nelson, John E. Bocknell, and Paul A. Hedlund, *Development and Refinement of Measures of Teaching Effectiveness* (Albany: The University of the State of New York, The State Education Department, 1956).

Loren R. Tomlinson, "Pioneer Studies in the Evaluation of Teaching," *Educational Research Bulletin,* Vol. XXXIV, No. 3 (March 9, 1955), 63–71.

William A. Watters, "Annotated Bibliography of Publications Related to Teacher Evaluation," *Journal of Experimental Education,* Vol. XXII, No. 4 (June 1954), 351–367.

[5] George B. Cutten, "The Professor and the Art of Teaching," *School and Society,* Vol. LXXXVII, No. 2146 (January 1959), 37.

related to teacher success in a wide variety of situations,"[6] was made on the basis of five different groups of teachers in the elementary and secondary schools of the nation, both public and private. This study has no counterpart for college teachers though the need for research in this area is clearly apparent.

In the absence of an adequate study of the qualifications generally associated with superior performance in the classroom, it may suffice to generalize that an effective college teacher has three major functions: a) the character building function; b) the informational function; and c) the research function. Success in fulfilling his role depends primarily upon the degree to which he conditions the intellects and attitudes of his students so that they will be receptive to learning, and upon his effectiveness in presenting his material in lesson units. Here his success in large measure will be contingent upon the following factors: a) appearance; b) personality; c) logical presentation and utilization of modern skills in presentation; d) ability to organize subject matter into meaningful and related units of instruction; and e) recognition of the individual differences and needs of his students. His effectiveness in reaching students will be conditioned markedly by his sympathy, helpfulness, sincerity, enthusiasm, and sense of humor.[7]

College teachers do not come from a common mold. Each is as unique an individual as his students are purported to be. Each has his own idiosyncrasies, strengths and weaknesses, desires and revulsions, which are normally reflected in his behavior.

Like the rest of humanity, college teachers soon learn from self-preservation to adapt their behavior to their environment. Therefore, if one possesses breadth and depth of scholarly commitment, and if he is also a poised, circumspect, erudite, and articulate person—one who, because of an air of resourcefulness, self-confidence, and unwavering integrity, inspires the confidence and respect of others—he will be able to generate a climate for learning.

Another quality vital in inter-personal communication is a sensitivity to the emotions of others coupled with a desire to preserve their emotional well-being. He who has it projects warmth, friendliness, interest, fairness, and kindness, entirely without delibera-

---

[6] Ben D. Wood, "Prefatory Note" in David G. Ryans, *Characteristics of Teachers: Their Description, Comparison and Appraisal* (Washington: American Council on Education, 1960), p. vii.

[7] Knapp, *op. cit.,* pp. 299–303.

tion, because all these are, essentially, responses to the needs of human beings. There is an obvious corollary here: since one cannot be self-conscious and at the same time conscious of others, the college teacher must be a reasonably selfless person. This quality cannot be imparted or cultivated in a preparation program.

A final criterion for successful college teaching might be termed "the inner joy for living," which is reflected in the enthusiasm of persons who have come to terms with the realities of life and enjoy every moment of it. Only adults who prize the joy of living can hope to understand, share, and preserve this quality in their students.

It is to be hoped that many, if not all, young college teachers may possess: 1) well reasoned personal and educational philosophies in terms of which they may evaluate their own attitudes and commitments; 2) strong sensitivity to the emotions of their fellow human beings; and 3) an abiding joy for living. Beyond these, it is further hoped that they will nurture their individuality rather than their commonality. This is basic, because greatness and conformity are notoriously ill-mated.

Professional qualifications. All professions have several requisites in common. There must be an intellectual commitment to excellence which: (1) recognizes challenging problems; (2) isolates relevant issues; (3) initiates and continues the search for truth and new knowledge; (4) welcomes critical appraisal; and (5) deplores specious intellectualism in any form.

Emotionally, one must see one's profession in terms of its relation and contribution to society. There must be an over-riding spirit of service, a sense of pride in perpetuating high standards of quality, a dedication to professional purpose which is not lessened by convenience, expediency, or pressure, and a feeling of kinship toward all who labor in the profession's common cause.

A person possessing such attitudes is not difficult to identify, especially when his profession is that of college teacher. He is marked by his unwillingness to be less than broadly and deeply educated. His respect for scholarship, by student or colleague, is as obvious as his contempt for pretension to erudition. No dogmatist, he may be dedicated to the preservation of the humanistic tradition entirely willing to re-define concepts and discard anachronistic principles in the light of contemporary social problems.

His emotional convictions are equally evident. His pride and support of his profession impel him to be critical of its shortcomings, while working to allay them. He is, therefore, well informed on how the profession as a whole is faring; well aware of the efforts being made by other members in its behalf; articulate in evaluating its progress; and unstinting in his own participation and contribution to it. The journals and books of other disciplines are familiar to him, and those of his own discipline are well known. His name is on the rosters of professional organizations, conferences, committees, and workshops. He takes an active position when issues arise to challenge the basic prerogatives of his profession—academic freedom, for example. He is, in brief, a professional teacher.

Personal satisfactions. Perhaps the most rewarding experience of a college teacher is the opportunity to work with students in a classroom setting. The happiness of a dedicated teacher in his career is made obvious through his mannerisms, his facial expressions, his stance, and his verbalizations. The difference in attitude between a master teacher who is a scholar, and a scholar who must perforce teach, is seldom lost upon students. The distinguishing characteristic of the master teacher is his compulsion to teach. His enthusiasm permeates every corner of the classroom. His sensitivity to the needs of individual students is reflected in the rapport such feeling engenders.

The modern college teacher is a member of a company of scholars. As such, he derives satisfaction from the opportunities afforded him to pursue his scholarly interests; but because of the prodigious amount of knowledge to be acquired, he is never completely satisfied. Equally rewarding is the challenge of teaching others what he has learned. As he opens the doors to new frontiers his students sense the excitement of discovery. Thus he may kindle the spirit of pure inquiry in his students and a new generation of scholars is born.

The activities of the teacher are primarily creative. He inquires into what seems to be unresolved, he assembles facts and data, he compiles statistics, he examines cause and effect, he searches deeply. Though his findings may be minute or important, these pursuits give him a feeling of accomplishment—of bringing a new discovery to the storehouse of knowledge.

Inspired by the vision of true scholarship, the modern college teacher attempts to comprehend the world of tomorrow as it takes shape today. In doing so, he perfects his techniques for exploring the past. Whether or not he succeeds in gaining wide recognition, he finds comfort in reading, questioning, and thinking. He thereby remains in the frontiers of knowledge in his specialization and transmits his findings with deep satisfaction to those of proved intellectual or operational capacity.

Functions of the College Teacher

Transmission of knowledge. There is no single definition that encompasses all the meanings of good teaching. To the layman, a teacher is a specialist who possesses techniques of telling or of showing how to do something. To the teacher below the college level of instruction, good teaching involves procedures for removing emotional blocks to learning; it may mean ways of selecting and organizing subject matter, or it may imply a capability for dealing with the difficult problems of attitudes and values. To the educator, whatever his level of assignment, teaching is to impart knowledge, information, skills, and concepts.

The art or science of college teaching has many gradations: it can be ineffective (shoddy, pedantic, boring, repetitive, irrelevant); or it can be highly effective (stimulating, inspiring, aesthetic, animated). Instruction can make learning exciting and interesting; on the other hand, it can fail completely to arouse students' curiosity or to motivate students to learn for themselves. Only masterful teaching achieves the desirable educational goals of instilling in each student the quenchless thirst for intellectual independence. A teacher develops this mastery only through long, persistent effort and self-appraisal.

There are indications that a renaissance of research on teacher education is underway. Experimental studies are probing new ways to accelerate learning, and methods to perfect the processes of acquiring and retaining knowedge are being tried. In the area of assessing student progress, psychometric skills have been developed for finding, measuring, motivating, and requiring individual intellectual excellence. Also being tried are new conditions of teaching that are intended to motivate and consequently shape perception. In another area, researchers are studying whether the quality of transmitting knowledge can be enhanced if the verbal performance employed in classroom discussions is improved.

These efforts are commendable in that scholar-teachers are attacking the problems of obsolescence in instruction. The findings to date augur well for the pursuit of excellence in teaching.

There is no subject so totally academic that it fails to evoke from students some opinions, values, judgments, or ideas. The teacher who accepts the responsibility for helping his students clarify their opinions is alert to revealing extemporizations by his students and eager to pursue the openings these offer for more serious discussions. Moreover, responsible teachers intentionally structure their courses so that students have the time that contemplation and effective expression demand. These students, more often than not, find themselves engaged in systematic feedback, that is, in testing the validity of their favorite opinions against the critical questioning of fellow students and teacher. The instructor's questions are designed ostensibly to help students clarify the students' understanding of the meaning of their own statements, and in so doing, clarify their own understanding. Typically, the questions require students: a) to define key remarks and state their underlying assumptions; b) to examine the validity of those assumptions in terms of supportable facts; c) to establish the origins of alleged facts; d) to predict outcomes or consequences; and e) to explore the bases for alternative or opposite viewpoints. Students are often asked to present their viewpoints in writing since this improves both their logic and their semantics.

One function of all college teachers is to assist students in gathering and comparing facts and ideas in such a manner that after the comparison is made, the student has established values to guide him as a person in coping with life's complexities. These values include acceptance of personal responsibility for one's own behavior, for one's continuous intellectual growth, and for whatever contribution to the welfare of humanity one is capable of making.

Much has been said of the usefulness of informal contacts between teachers and students. College teachers serve as class and club advisers, guidance counselors, tutors, and resource persons, and in various roles in which mutual respect and rapport between teacher and student can be established. On a still more informal basis are social gatherings of faculty and students at teas, dinners, dances, receptions, and in the homes of faculty in the "tea and sympathy" tradition. Sometimes these meetings are memorable occasions for students; at other times they are bores—or worse, periods of strain and embarrassment, depending upon the teacher or teachers involved.

The most essential ingredient in a successful meeting of teacher and student is a commonality of interests. Where there is interest, there is also opinion and, to varying degrees, knowledge. Where the teacher has little or no idea of a student's concern, he is likely to find the discussion somewhat one-sided—his side. In the meantime his student will be writhing inwardly as he tries to follow the teacher's train of thought, to fight down dread of the moment when he must make an intelligent response or contrive a graceful retreat.

Where such informal meetings are school policy, the less socially gifted teachers may suffer the same agonies as their students before the sporadic outbursts of remarks, the stilted inanities, and the long pauses which pass for counseling are mercifully interrupted.

But where teachers and students meet for a predetermined purpose to which they are prepared to contribute, personal anxieties and inadequacies are sublimated and conversation flows naturally. As confidence is thus built between students and teachers, the conversational range broadens and deepens—and rapport is established.

Withal, the classroom remains the basic educational situation and there students need not display social prowess.

Generation of knowledge. Blake has described the master teacher as being

> . . . intellectually curious, objective and dispassionate in dealing with Truth

while

> . . . 'clinically' as it were, he ministers to one of the most universal and serious afflictions of the human mind—ignorance.[8]

Teaching demands breadth and depth of learning and free inquiry for the teacher must constantly seek to expand and enrich his insights and understandings. Beyond this, the modern college

---

[8] John A. Blake, "The Master Teacher: A New Type of Specialist," AAUP *Bulletin,* Vol. XL, No. 2 (June 1954), 247.

teacher needs know-how in other areas; he needs knowledge of himself, of his students, and of the society in which he serves. He must study to become more than a purveyor of cultural heritage or of skills and concepts; he must become sensitive, critically perceptive, to the reasons for directing his instruction to meet the interests, abilities, and needs of his students.

Teachers who engage in self-directed search for truth probe all the available resources at their command. In their own fields of specialization they learn from their faculty colleagues and from experts across the land and around the world. They learn from the written record—from contributions to knowledge published regularly in professional journals, proceedings, research reports, and monographs. Scientific propositions, independent discoveries, theoretical ideas, and findings of significant studies are reported in regional, national, and international conferences. Papers delivered in conventions are made available to conferees at professional gatherings. Communications by post, telephone, telegraph, and television may eclipse the more formal kinds of meetings. Colleagues often convene in one another's homes to pursue informally their own scholarly interests.

Pursuit of truth. For many centuries teachers have drawn upon their own creativity to advance knowledge. They build upon all that they have learned through study and from others as they attempt to make contributions. They explore and experiment, applying to their own projects what others have discovered; or they attempt entirely new ventures which, as investigators, they have theorized and designed. They become intrigued by hypotheses and delve ever more deeply for solutions within a scientifically controlled structure. Some engage in pure research—the Aladdin's lamp of the Twentieth Century, the magic word in the modern American lexicon. In earlier years, citizens readily accepted the pronouncements of persons of alleged authority. A college teacher, by virtue of his profession, was presumed to be an authority. Today such naïveté is amusing. Presumably the American public, now more sophisticated, no longer is gulled by mere authority. People want facts, figures, scientific proof, and documentation. They respect research, so research becomes a new authority figure.

There are methods of research appropriate to each academic discipline. College teachers are conversant with these methods not because they once read or heard of them, but because they employ them routinely. Otherwise, the classroom soon becomes sterile; "old" knowledge languishes for want of new concepts, horizons, and knowledge; and both students and teachers are without criteria for judging significant research, thus adding to intellectual stagnation. Large numbers of the profession's leaders recognize this fact, as is indicated by the vast numbers of research programs underway in colleges and universities, and by the frequency with which research reports appear on the agenda of professional conferences.

Guba states that the indispensable requirements for quality research are capable people, commitment to the problem at hand, support and encouragement for neophytes as well as for established researchers, time, resources, recognition, reward, and communication.[9] Significantly, he maintains that "Research will be increasingly more complex and diverse and will require new skills and competence as well as new resources and arrangements."[10] One of the most challenging practices he mentions is the encouragement of co-operative research projects and interdisciplinary research teams.

Academic circles are excited about the feasibility of establishing regional information centers for the use of scholar-teachers and graduate students. Conceivably, the optical scanners and digital computers at these centers would catalog, digest, and store appropriate items of information from reports, research studies, and literature. Colleges and universities would subscribe to the services of regional centers and be tied to them by data transmission lines. In short order, a scholar could obtain electronically all the pertinent and timely information needed in his particular area of research or writing.

Theoretically, scholars employing computer technology may begin to harness the newly generated knowledge at a phenomenal rate. It has been estimated that more than one million technical papers are published throughout the world each year. As this expansion of knowledge continues, researchers can no longer keep

---

[9] Egon G. Guba, ed., "Principles for Research in Education and Illustrative Practices," American Association of Colleges for Teacher Education *Bulletin,* Vol. XIV, No. 11 (December 20, 1961).

[10] *Ibid.,* p. 4.

abreast of frontiers of learning without employing these more efficient developments in the dissemination of research.

Currently differences of opinion are expressed about the mixing of research activities and teaching responsibilities. Some educators hold that the two are mutually exclusive—that teaching and research present an "either/or" situation. This point of view holds that a professor either does research and neglects his teaching—if he is so unfortunate as to be assigned classes that must be taught— or he teaches his classes and has no time for research, or interest in it. There is a widespread tendency to deplore the increasing involvement of university faculty members in research, presumably to the detriment of the service required by students who come to get an education.

A contrasting point of view holds that teaching and research are not only compatible activities, but that they actually reinforce each other. The classroom teaching of the instructor engaged actively in research is likely to be vital and challenging, rather than only a dull rehashing of the long existent contents of the storehouse of knowledge. It is claimed that ideas about research that ought to be done, or about means of carrying on investigative projects, come to the teacher as he prepares for his classes, as he meets problems raised by the alert minds of his students, and as, from his efforts to communicate knowledge, he senses the gaps in the evidence that ought to be filled by further investigation.

The arguments on both sides of the question are formidable. No pat solution can be offered to the problem of how research and teaching can be carried on most effectively in a given institution by a single faculty body. In the large university there are likely to be some faculty members highly gifted in research, who are so uninterested in teaching and so lacking in pedagogical skill that they should not be assigned undergraduate classes. Such faculty members may confine their teaching, if any, to the more advanced graduate courses, in classes composed of mature students who can serve effectively as collaborators in the professors' research projects. The market places a high value on the service of researchers, and the faculty member with this kind of talent will likely advance rapidly in salary and academic rank; and he will be offered attractive opportunities at other universities.

Equally, it may be presumed that there are in most colleges

and universities some faculty members who are highly skilled as teachers and very successful in their classroom performance, but who lack interest in and ability to do research, when that term is defined as original investigation leading to a significant increase in knowledge. Such faculty members clearly should not be forced into going through the motions of research, boring themselves, taking time that they might better devote to their students, and producing nothing of value. Instead, they should be encouraged to spend their energies on their teaching and other contacts with students. The encouragement should be both in the recognition accorded them by their colleagues and by suitable promotions in academic rank and salary.

The relative emphasis to be placed on teaching and research is a matter of institutional policy. In a university with a prestigious graduate school, the emphasis may quite likely be heavily on research. In an undergraduate college of liberal arts, the emphasis is quite generally on teaching, with research considered as a somewhat incidental function, though it may be given some encouragement. A young scholar seeking a position on the faculty of an institution of higher education should inquire carefully about its policy, so that he may associate himself where the academic climate is compatible with his own interests and talents. In most universities, and probably in a majority of the undergraduate colleges, the announced policy is to encourage both research and effective classroom teaching. The actual distribution of emphasis, however, may differ considerably from the policy stated in the college catalog or the faculty handbook.

Hopefully, the two functions of research and teaching can be and are combined successfully. In general, the researcher has an intense desire to communicate the results of his investigations. He commonly likes to discuss his plans for studies, particularly with those who can criticize or suggest improvements in his research design. A class of alert students furnishes an excellent audience for this sort of communication. The professor deeply interested in research must, in the classroom, restrain his enthusiasm for it somewhat, and must fit his presentation to the maturity of his students. But an actual excursion now and then into the realm of knowledge just over the horizon is both refreshing and exhilarating, especially to the abler students.

The other kind of professor, who is mainly interested in teaching, can also profit greatly by some investigative activity. If he is not particularly interested in research in his own academic field, he certainly should be sensitive to the possibilities of studies directed toward the improvement of his own teaching. Which of two different ways of organizing the content he is trying to teach evokes the better response from his students? Can his procedures for evaluating student accomplishment be improved in reliability and validity? Research on such problems is likely to be profitable, and just as stimulating mentally as research related directly to the teacher's academic discipline. Through research of this kind by actual classroom teachers, general knowledge may be effectively extended in the fields of college instructional procedures, organization of subject matter, and evaluation of student achievement and behavior patterns. The college teacher who conducts such studies, and shares his findings through the publication of reports or the presentation of papers, makes a "contribution to knowledge" fully as significant as that of a colleague who finds evidence to correct an immaterial error in a traditionally accepted historical fact, or who discovers some hitherto unknown facet of the life or writings of an obscure eighteenth-century poet.

While there are opportunities in higher education for the research assistant who may do no teaching, and for the teaching fellow who does no research, the ideal is the teacher-scholar who combines both abilities. Most appointing officers in American colleges and universities eagerly seek the faculty member who has a lively interest in his students and in the teaching process and also an inquiring mind that is never satisfied with the existing store of knowledge but always desirous of extending it.

CHAPTER III

A Climate for Learning

To convert exuberant adolescents and overworked adults into a "company of scholars" is no small task—yet this is the mandate set for every college and graduate school, the challenge facing every college teacher.

Life is, for youth, full of fascinating things—sports, clothes, friends, parties, love; full of worrisome things—failure, rejection, loss of those held dear, inadequacy; full of irksome things—physical imperfections, parental restrictions, the slowness with which one becomes adult. None but the most unrealistic college teacher could expect many students to assume the role of serious-minded scholars at the undergraduate level.

For the adult, life is also full of fascinating things—family, profession, friends, colleagues, hobbies, politics; and worrisome things—insecurity, illness, loss of opportunities or social status; and irksome things—remarks one ought not to have made, actions one did not take, and the speed with which one grows old. None but the most unrealistic professor could expect all these adult graduate students to emulate his own single-minded dedication to professional scholarship.

What, then, comprises the legitimate expectation of scholarship for these two groups?

At the undergraduate level, students should develop a commitment to scholarship, a "tool kit" of skills and knowledge, and possibly a habitual curiosity. At the graduate level, the commitment should be renewed, the "tool kit" more substantially equipped, and the curiosity channeled into productive paths of inquiry—provided the prevailing climate is conducive to learning.

Climates conducive to learning vary markedly from classroom to classroom and from institution to institution, if one may judge by the critical comments of students. This variety of response has led educators to attempt to identify the components of a conducive climate.

Reports of studies of educational climate now in progress seem to indicate a new and fruitful field for social scientists. This field should increase in importance as anthropologists, sociologists, psychologists, and psychiatrists involved in research in college-teacher evaluation find ways to coordinate their efforts and interests in the thinking and learning processes, and in the changes occurring in student behavior during college years. Currently, much attention is directed toward perfecting instruments to quantify the social forces that affect the outcomes of teaching, and to isolate and describe the nature of as many non-cognitive elements as possible.

Changes within individuals between admission to college and intellectual maturity, and the effect of these changes on learning in general, are being studied in order to determine if these changes may be directly attributable to college attendance. The total absence of change within some students, a dramatic, painful, and observable phenomenon, has received wide attention. Researchers have isolated several causal factors. A few are purely physical. Uncomfortable seating arrangements, poor acoustics, improper room temperature and ventilation, as well as inadequate lighting, can mar the effect of a teacher's performance. Therefore, college instructors as well as administrators are increasingly alert to these physical factors. The physical health of students affects their receptivity and participation, so student health departments play a part in creating a climate conducive to learning.

The institution's guidance and counseling services can also play an integral part in improving the climate for learning, since one or another of the worries or irritations mentioned at the start of this chapter can also interfere with the learning process.

The most virulent instances of non-learning arise from teacher-student relationships. Whether or not a teacher will be able to help a student learn hinges as much on the rapport which is established between them as upon the quality of his presentation and the appropriateness of his procedures and illustrations.

As he addresses a class, a professor is appraised by each student in it. His appearance, manner, expressions, gestures, choice of words, opinions, attitudes, and commitments project to each student an impression of the professor as a person. A positive impression makes the student receptive to what the professor seeks to communicate, and learning may begin. When the impression is negative the student is either resistant or disturbed, and learning is obstructed.

While there is as yet no infallible list of behavior patterns and appearances which guarantee student receptivity to professors, a few reasonably successful principles have emerged from the many studies conducted in the area. The college teacher should exhibit an intellectual integrity which precludes both dogmatism and sham-scholarship. The teacher's function is to teach, not to confound. He who is truly knowledgeable can afford to speak clearly and simply. It is also the teacher's function to implant within students a self-generating interest in expanding the horizons of knowledge. This cannot be done when there are only "irrefutable facts." Human progress has been made only because some men doubted the "facts" of their time.

It has been said that a man who talks long enough reveals his innermost being. A teacher runs considerable risk, since talking is his *modus operandi*. Initially he may not be quite as revealing as this statement implies, for he tries at first to project himself according to his conception of his role; but as the semester progresses the teacher's actual disposition tends to emerge subtly. Therefore a teacher would do well to "be himself" in the classroom, eschewing the mannerisms and attitudes of his own most unforgettable professors or those which he believes comprise the professor image. Affected postures do not weather the wear and tear of daily classroom exposure. If the teacher's attitudes vary from those he tries to project, the inconsistent behavior which results can confuse and disturb students, thus impairing the climate for learning.

College teachers who respect the intellectual potential of their students and who recognize that their own superiority is based largely on experience and maturity are most likely to enhance the climate for learning. The lively exchange of ideas and the students' enthusiasm for attacking problems independently, usually found in the classrooms of such teachers, are proof of the students' confidence in themselves, in one another, and in their professors. Notably absent from these classrooms are the sarcasm and superciliousness which inevitably accompany the pseudo-intellectual professor, and which breed defeatism and boredom among students.

Finally, college teachers are generally dedicated by nature to building a better world. This is clearly reflected in the professional literature. Part of almost every conference, convention, address, and article is devoted to a consideration of ways to change students into better human beings through their college experiences. Oddly enough, this laudable impulse can frequently create a resistance, depending upon a student's earlier development. New values are frequently hard-gotten.

The nearly universal tendency of human beings to resist change is attributed to the threat which change implies. In the case of the college professor who would influence student values and morals, direct frontal attack is foredoomed. Students whose values and moral commitments agree with the professor's will be reassuringly vocal. Students whom he would like to reach will feel threatened because they believe they have lost his respect. This damages their self-esteem and the values by which they have ordered their security are shaken in direct proportion to the degree of respect with which they have held him. Therefore, students will reject both him and his propositions. It is important that the teacher learn his students' commitments as individuals, provide the experiences peculiar to their needs, and demonstrate the interrelatedness and possible extensions of particular points of view—but he should not draw students' conclusions for them.

If a college teacher has these four attributes—intellectual integrity, genuineness in that he shows his true character and feelings in speech and action, respect for students' intellectual potential, and wise dedication to student attainment of scholarly and moral ideals—he can naturally begin to structure his classroom endeavors so that:

1. course content is selected on the basis of its intrinsic worth, not for its impressive difficulty;
2. each student is guided toward goals appropriate to him as an individual;
3. success is measured in terms of the quality of a student's decisions, objective judgments, human behavior, and social contributions as well as his recall of subject matter, high grades, and academic honors;
4. new and creative ways of imparting knowledge are constantly being tried to facilitate learning at various stages of readiness, to render presentations livelier and more interesting, and to ascertain the most appropriate techniques for particular kinds of content;

5. student verbalization is not a synonym for mimicry of the teacher, but it involves the ability to state one's premises with the coherence and individuality which accompany understanding, personal involvement, and commitment;

6. learning experiences are inherently satisfying, and situations challenge the learner to utilize and test prior concepts and experiences in order to accommodate and comprehend new materials;

7. the informality of colleagues engaged in a mutually absorbing endeavor prevails; spontaneous feedback and immediate association of ideas tend to augment a student's understanding and, incidentally, to raise the state of his morale;

8. focus is never upon minutiae at the expense of a large frame of reference or relationship, for the data and ideas of the moment are taught best within the perspective of a larger whole;

9. each student is actively encouraged to venture and then test his hypotheses;

10. presentations by the teacher utilize audio-visual aids and modern media of instruction.

Where students are observed eagerly grasping the initiative for their own learning, there one concludes that the climate is indeed "conducive."

Instructional Methods and Materials

At the point of the selection of appropriate methods and materials of instruction a teacher's quality is most easily assessed and his probability of success most accurately projected. His approach to this task reveals his philosophy of education, his command of his discipline, his knowledge of students (his own in particular) and of how they learn.

If one may judge by the classroom performance of some college teachers, deans and department chairmen are not universally aware of this criterion. Neither are they aware of the instructional improvement that could be made if faculty members were required to present and justify their proposed methods and materials of instruction before the first class meeting. How many beginning college teachers, for example, would have the temerity to confide to their department chairmen that their classroom performance will consist in merely summarizing a few chapters of the textbook?

It is the responsibility of academic deans and department chairmen to facilitate the preparation of college teachers for their professional responsibilities: (a) by giving early notice of teaching assignments and by carefully allotting other encroaching activities in order to allow the teacher maximum preparation time; and (b) by making facilities, equipment, and materials easily accessible.

Time and money are well spent in maintaining an up-to-date catalog of available audio-visual materials and by apprising teachers of new resources. Non-use or partial use of these materials is wasteful. The orientation of every new teacher should include introduction to the location, operation, and availability of instructional materials by the staff members in charge of them. Otherwise, a loss of teacher time and a lessening of effectiveness result as these resource materials lie idle. A final reason for the requirement that teachers advance proposals of methods and materials is that this affords department heads an opportunity to suggest instructional materials that may be used to amplify and enforce learning.

Making right choices to insure effective instruction. If he has been given the kind of orientation suggested above, the teacher then faces the necessity for making a few critical decisions, the first of which is, "What am I going to teach?"

If the teacher is not to bog both himself and his students down in a mire of minutiae, he must establish the learning priorities he desires and construct his course outlines accordingly. A relevant question he might ask is, "What do they (the students) need to know?" With such a perspective, a history teacher is not likely to focus the attention of his freshmen students upon the details and dates of events, at the expense of a sensitivity to relative impact of events upon civilization.

A second appropriate question is, "How much should I teach?" The difference between this and the first question might be clearer if the word *tell* is substituted for *teach.*

In the past it has often been assumed that a teacher's primary function was to tell his students what he knew, and to let them use the acquired knowledge, facts, and information as they would. The pendulum has swung the other way, and thoughtful educators now insist that students should largely find knowledge for themselves and that the teacher should give few if any answers. This position is based on the assumption that active learning occurs only when the student becomes excited and is motivated to learn.

Extremes have a way of being self-defeating and, in the final analysis, most educators would agree that teachers must maintain a reasonable balance between knowledge which they present, and knowledge which students gain for themselves. A teacher may achieve the perspective needed by posing these questions: "What can students learn most efficiently on their own?" and "Which important learnings are students unable to attain efficiently for themselves and are, therefore, within my province to present as the teacher?"

Having determined the course content and his own and the students' areas of responsibility, the teacher is ready to select his methods and materials. It should be noted that the term "methods" is plural. The earnest efforts of countless researchers have failed to establish any single teaching method as being demonstrably superior to another.

The term *teaching* is deceptive in that it appears to connote a single cognitive experience, when actually it comprises a range of experiences relative to an objective. In the entire course, a teacher may use many methods and different materials to improve the learning of concepts. The best method is that which most effectively and efficiently accomplishes the task at hand. Any method and any material is only as good as the instructor utilizing it. For each lesson the method of procedure and related materials should be selected with care.

The lecture method. Over the years, experience and experimentation have shown several methods to be peculiarly effective for fulfilling particular teaching tasks. The most venerable and omnipresent of these is the lecture method. Its advocates cite these advantages: (1) it transmits information quickly and concisely; (2) it accommodates large groups of students; and (3) it allows the students to react and the instructor to respond to their reactions. Its opponents counter: (1) the students too often do not learn because they are passive participants in the process; (2) the larger the group the fewer the number of verbalized feedback reactions of students; and (3) the lecture is beamed at the *average* students in the group, boring the superior and confusing the poorer students. Withal, the fact remains that a brilliant lecturer can stimulate students' intellectual participation, whether or not it is verbalized, and generate learning. There is far more to a good lecture than brilliant extemporization. A few hallmarks for excellence are:

1. that in the content of his lecture, the instructor develops under-standings, concepts, or information that students could otherwise obtain only with great difficulty and little hope of success; he must do this by design, not happenstance;
2. that the lecturer attempts to have his students recognize the value of his communication in terms of their own objectives;
3. that the lecturer speaks; rather than orate: he must speak with enthusiasm, candor, clarity, and humor, and draw upon the students' experiences for his illustrations; and
4. that, as the preceding criteria imply, the lecturer has taken the trouble to know his students personally, and, as director of the learning situation, has made provision for individual differences.

While there are undoubtedly some professors who subscribe only to a pure lecture method, many variations make the basic lecture a bit smoother as an operational technique and alleviate some of its natural shortcomings.[1]

Actual objects, films, slides, and tape recordings do much to relieve the monotony of a lecture, as well as to enlighten and enrich student's concepts. The teacher should preview instructional aids before they are used in the class to determine their worth and to ascertain their purpose and the significant concepts to be stressed.

It behooves the college teacher to be self-reliant. Knowing how to operate the modern instruments and automated machines can spare him many an ulcerating hour of tinkering and stalling while he waits for someone to come and deal with the recalcitrant equipment.

The discussion method.　A second major teaching method is discussion. Where the lecture is essentially a monologue, discussion implies a dialogue. Here the responsibility for communication is shared by the teacher and the students. The teacher assumes responsibility for initiating the topic of discussion, providing students with common experiences upon which to base their participation, stimulating students to think critically, keeping the discussions from drifting into tangential dead-ends, and reminding students of where the group has progressed in relation to their stated goals. The students assume responsibility for contributing their individual thinking, investigations, and conclusions to the group effort.

There are numerous variations of the discussion method, includ-

---

[1] See Wilbert McKeachie, *Teaching Tips: A Guidebook for the Beginning College Teacher* (Ann Arbor: George Wahr Publishing Co., 1960), pp. 15–16.

ing the Socratic approach, the forum, the panel, the seminar, and the tutorial method.

The laboratory method. A third major teaching method, the laboratory method, is an extension of the learn-by-doing concept. It provides the students with "first hand experience in observing and manipulating the materials of a science."[2]

Educators disagree on the relative merits of the demonstration and the experimental laboratory methods. In the demonstration method, the outcome of the procedure is predicted and the procedure itself is rigidly structured by the manual or by the teacher. This applies whether the student demonstrates for himself or the teacher demonstrates for the class. Derided as the "cookbook" method, it has several obvious shortcomings, not the least of which is that it does not encourage the student to create, reason, or criticize, but has him merely follow directions. Too often, it may circumscribe the possibilities of the students' realizing the principles involved.

A demonstration is a legitimate means of communicating some techniques to students. The teacher must distinguish, however, between those principles which are best demonstrated and those which are best discovered—which brings us to the experimental laboratory method.

Here, the conclusions are presumably no longer predetermined. The teacher helps each student formulate his problems, provides the necessary background knowledge and experience, and suggests procedures; the student sets up the necessary apparatus, carries out the procedures, and draws his own conclusions. Later, by reviewing procedures and conclusions, the teacher can help each student clarify the relationships of his unit experiments to the larger frame of reference of a scientific principle.

Selecting a focus. Whichever methods the college teacher utilizes to implement a particular teaching task, he will have to select a focus for his presentation if the efforts he and the students expend are to have direction. Case studies, problem solving, and projects are examples of such foci:

1. Case studies afford students opportunities to analyze the circumstances and components of concrete situations. They are able

----

2 *Ibid.,* p. 51.

to apply principles creatively in suggesting possible courses of action. In some instances, the cases are merely presented to the students for their analysis, suggestions, and discussion. In others, students compile their own case histories, analyze them, and present their recommendations to the group for discussion. Still others give students the opportunity to implement and follow up their recommendations, as in some remedial reading courses wherein advanced students work in a clinical situation with young children who are retarded readers.

2. Problem-solving, provided that the problems are genuine, challenging, and capable of being solved, offers the best focus for students' efforts yet discovered. The problems are sometimes volunteered by the students; many are posited by the teachers; and others are inherent in the subject itself. The teacher usually attempts to introduce those most closely allied to the learning goals of the group. This is not difficult if students are aware of and in agreement with both the procedure for problem-solving and the goals. The most obvious way of effecting this is to involve students in the formulation of goals, and in the determination of the route for attaining them.

3. When group effort is focused upon a project, the activity is much the same as in problem solving—formulating the problem or project, collecting relevant data, proposing solutions, testing them, and evaluating outcomes. Additionally, a delegation of responsibility and a final articulation and correlation of efforts is involved.

Groupings to enhance learning. Throughout the country college teachers, aware that the demand for higher education will increase, are wondering whether the end product—the graduating senior—can be produced en masse with improved knowledge, modern skills, creative abilities, and value standards.

Experimental attempts to organize students for purposes of large-group instruction, individual study, and small-group discussion would appear to hold the answer to the challenge of both quantity and quality. Such groupings do not need to lose sight of the consistent need for effective teaching, for selection of appropriate instructional methods and materials, and for giving students increased responsibility for an evaluation of their own learning.

Dimensions of Leadership

In one's field of specialization. Young college teachers possess a precious legacy of knowledge and ideas, generated by the great teachers who preceded them. Inherited also is the responsibility for creative utilization, expansion, and improvement of this legacy. Each generation has its productive scholars, who take up the standard of the greats in their field, and go forward to the ultimate benefit of themselves, their profession, and the rest of mankind.

Whatever his discipline, each outstanding college teacher shares a circumstance in common with his fellows: his contribution to society's fund of ideas and knowledge is a concomitant of his continuing process of learning—it is not an end product. This is a most important point for the young college teacher to ponder. To achieve pre-eminence is not to ascend a peak in darkness to find the summit unaccountably endowed with light. Similarly, one's contribution to knowledge is not dependent upon attainment of a graduate degree or a professorship in a desired institution, association with the "right" people, or even a specified amount of experience or intelligence. One may obtain all these and wait in vain for a single significant inspiration. It is in the genuine, purposeful pursuit of knowledge, in the continuing process of learning, in the creative response to the challenge of a problem, that inspired conceptualizations are formed that later may become contributions to knowledge.

Today's college students are evidently quite aware of the continuous nature of the learning process, judging by the increasing percentages of graduating seniors who enroll for further advanced study. It speaks well for the college teaching profession that more students than ever before take up post-doctoral studies, and that increased attention is being given to areas of an interdisciplinary character. This interest results from a spirit of pure inquiry that is developed in a large number of bright undergraduates and in whom the probing of possible theories becomes imbued. Upon graduation, these students continue to be motivated into examining more closely the broad spectrum of problems encountered in a variety of subject areas.

In this technological age, continuing education is necessary in many occupations. The widespread educational programs sponsored by industry that employs the instructional and consultive services of college faculties are evidence of this need. One author has aptly compared the intellectual demands upon college teachers of the thirties and upon those of two or three decades later by noting the size of the physics handbooks. The amount of information accrued in fifteen centuries was doubled in a mere twenty years.[4] College teaching is no profession for the mediocre, the haven seekers, or the apathetic.

In shaping institutional policy. College teaching has always benefited from the inspired leaders produced by the "great" institutions of higher education. But today the need is more urgent than ever for many excellent institutions, not just a few "great" ones.

It is easy to abdicate responsibility for educational leadership on the grounds that the larger, more famed, and affluent institutions are better able to exercise it, just as it is easy to attribute the shortcomings of one's own institution to the fact that it lacks the size, endowment, and name attractions of those of the "Ivy League." But those who do so overlook the important fact that an institution's greatness today is not the legacy of past glory but the product of present effort. Any institution is only as good as its present members choose to make it. Yesterday's scholars, teachers, philosophers, and administrators are gone. However great their contributions to their institutions and the teaching profession during their lifetimes, they continue to have influence only where those who came after them choose to carry on in the same scholarly spirit. The intellectual leaders of the past have fulfilled their responsibilities. They have initiated the efforts necessary to their time. It remains for today's members of the teaching profession to continue their elders' work, and to initiate the new efforts necessary to the times.

Fulfillment of this responsibility demands of each member of the academic community—whether in the role of teacher, scholar, researcher, or administrator—intellectual honesty, integrity, and participation in the evaluation and support of his colleagues' efforts. Such contributions are made continuously in colleges and

---

[4] W. G. Torpey, "The Role of Higher Education in Improving the Utilization of Scientific and Technical Manpower," an unpublished address delivered before the 17th Annual National Conference on Higher Education, Chicago, March 3, 1962. A synopsis appears in *Current Issues in Higher Education* (Washington: Association for Higher Education, 1962), pp. 121–24.

universities all over the country, and promise solutions to many of higher education's growing problems.

Increased attention and respect are being given the individual student's potential; students of different intellectual strengths are being recruited along with the academically gifted—the creative, the articulate, the musical, even the "odd." At Yale research opportunities are being offered as early as the freshman year to students who seem capable. Curricula comprised of courses utilizing faculty from more than one discipline are expanding the academic horizons of the students.

The foregoing are but a few of the efforts of educators in response to the unending challenges of the times—challenges that continually test the caliber of each institution in the quality of its faculty's response.

In participation in community activities. There are few colleges or universities so munificently blessed with endowments that they are independent of other support. For the vast majority, the image which they present to the public is more than an asset—it is an instrument of survival. It is incumbent upon each staff member to help create a positive image through his off-campus activities.

The public is the source from which come students, endowments, gifts, legislative appropriations, and moral support for the whole enterprise of higher education. Through his participation in civic affairs, the educator can focus the interest of laymen upon those areas of education which require assistance, financial and otherwise. Conversely, the public can become aware of the problems which educators are best qualified to solve. The modern college teacher-scholar is also a citizen; he cannot afford the luxury of an "ivory tower."

The college teacher in his role as citizen may be well known to his neighbors, who observe his behavior in daily contacts. As they find him satisfactory or otherwise they accordingly judge not only his institution, but the teaching profession and higher education in general. Thus college teachers have many opportunities to enhance public regard for themselves, their institution, and their profession.

In developing skill in interpersonal relations. At some time in his budding career the young college teacher becomes aware that the academic community is also an aggregation of human beings, subject to the same moral and ethical lapses which plague the rest of mankind. He will probably be either shocked or relieved by this realization, depending upon his prior conception of the nature of college teachers and whether or not the particular lapse which he observes corresponds to one of his own weaknesses. This phenomenon is worth mentioning because these teachers are charged with the responsibility for perfecting, insofar as is possible, the youth of a nation—a task which necessitates the sublimation of baser impulses and the projection of all which is good within them. The education of young people is a joint task, shared by all who teach them, and demanding the best which each individual can bring to the common endeavor; but the lapses of some members have created factions which seriously impair the effectiveness of the total educational program in many institutions. Young college teachers must decide whether they are going to join a particular faction or attempt to unite warring groups. It is not whether they do one or the other which will determine the course of higher education, but how. If a faction is considered as a group sharing a common interest or viewpoint in general opposition to another, college teachers can scarcely avoid belonging to one or another or even several such "factions."

Factionalism, in the sense of lively intellectual exchange, is constructive, since opposing viewpoints serve to sharpen the scrutiny of principles and assumptions, whether the purpose be defensive or offensive. But factionalism can be an utterly demoralizing and destructive force when it cuts off communication between opposing groups. Somehow "they" can invoke an unbridled antagonism and indefinable alarm which the most formidable "you" is incapable of provoking.

The concept of "togetherness" has been the butt of many jokes in recent years, but it can be a potent factor in promoting harmony within a faculty. An administrator who utilizes every opportunity to bring the members of various disciplines together, to work on some institutional problem or to attend informal social and professional affairs, contributes much to the morale of his institution. People who work together, who talk and laugh with each other and who share their problems and their projects, usually come to understand and, often, to respect each other. When such conditions prevail, institutional problems are more easily solved, uncomplicated by the misunderstanding of motives which bedevil strangers holding opposite views.

Inimical to interdisciplinary or any other kind of harmony is the element of competition where its corollary is threat. In itself, competition is unavoidable and not entirely undesirable. In a profession where intellectual excellence is essential, the competition for it is keen. Where such competition results in greater numbers of fine scholarly contributions, it enhances the profession. There are circumstances, however, in which the competitive aspect becomes so exaggerated as to shift the efforts of some faculty members from a professional to a political plane. In such instances, power politics, sniping, "apple-polishing," caucusing, and other divisive behavior may become apparent. Realizing this, many administrators minimize the competitive aspect wherever possible. Others are faced with situations about which they can do little, as in institutions where varsity athletic coaches are pressured by the need to produce conference champions. Some schools, colleges, or departments within a university complex are direct victims of competition, forced to operate on inadequate budgets because funds are channeled consistently by officers in authority to more esteemed operations.

Occasionally, institutional administrators are accused of showing favoritism to individuals, departments, colleges, or schools. Where this impression prevails the effects are usually disastrous. There is resistance to both the administrator and the allegedly favored; there is a breakdown in communication and, often, a loss of job efficiency. The accuser's shortcomings may be obliterated in his own eyes in the light of such "unfair competition," and finally the charge may change from "X is favored" to "I am the victim of discrimination." No one emerges unscathed from such situations. Because of the competitive pressures which all college teachers must face to some degree, administrators are understandably anxious to select faculty members who exhibit mature emotional balance and self-confidence along with professional integrity.

For young college teachers, the following hints may prove helpful in establishing mutually satisfactory relations with other members of the academic fraternity:

1. *With colleagues on the faculty of one's institution:*
   Each person regards himself as sincere, honorable, possessed of some professional ability and background, and a contributor of something of lasting value to the students served. And "I" am not the only one who is not in error in this belief.

2. *With members of the administrative staff of one's institution:*

It saves considerable time and inestimable wear on the nerves of both administrators and teachers when the latter proceed on the assumption that their best is abundantly adequate, and that their administrators are less concerned with their minor weaknesses than with their major strengths.

3. *With scholars everywhere who share one's field of academic interest:*

In the academic community a man is a scholar only as he learns from his fellows, acknowledges their influence upon thinking, seeks out for himself some new, valuable knowledge and contributes it to the general fund of knowledge upon which others may build.

4. *With educational statesmen throughout the country who are concerned about the total problems of higher education in a dynamic society:*

An enterprise as vast as American higher education is cannot exist without those educators who focus upon its immediate tasks and problems. Neither can it progress without those who observe its topography in broader perspective and those who scan its horizons, thereby affording orientation and purpose to those concerned with the immediate work—provided that the latter occasionally look up from their tasks and take heed.

CHAPTER IV

Preparation for College Teaching

There is no universal pattern of preparation for college teaching in the United States and the programs actually followed assume many different forms.

Ideally, for the efficient use of a student's time, talent, and money, the pre-service preparation should be designed in orderly, carefully planned steps. The most economical use of the high level talent needed for college teaching would require the program of preparation to be completed without interruptions or delays, to produce the fully prepared teacher in the minimum of elapsed time after entrance to the program. Realistically, however, the current need for college teachers is especially acute in certain fields, and graduate students are often tempted to interrupt their training in order to take an especially attractive position that is offered them. Thus, the law of supply and demand tends to defeat the establishment of a common pattern of preparation.

The program of preparation for college teaching, stretched out over a period of years, is expensive. The amount of financial aid, in the form of scholarships, fellowships, and loans, while on the increase, is still inadequate to meet the needs of those preparing for college teaching in many fields. Students who lack financial resources to complete all degree requirements often find it advisable to postpone the completion of their preparation until after they have actually begun service as a college or university teacher. Most institutions generously allow leaves of absence to their younger faculty members for the completion of residence requirements, the writing of a dissertation, or other final phases of the work for the doctor's degree. An arrangement of this sort facilitates the beginner's acquiring the doctor's degree after his entrance to teaching.

Another deterrent to the development of a universally accepted pattern of preparation of college teachers is the lack of research in this fertile field of investigation. Although extensive experimentation to weigh the merits of automated devices in cognition and in instruction is now in progress, little attention is being given to such areas as evaluating the quality of teaching, determining whether institutional objectives are realistic and meaningful, or discovering whether prescribed curricula are producing graduates who are performing effectively and measuring up to announced goals.

College teaching would be enhanced greatly if more professors had the interest and the time to be involved in this type of inquiry. Prior to the 1940's, the temper of students was of something less than concern to college professors. But the irreverent candor of "G.I." students after World War II, often a source of mirth to the public and chagrin to college officers and administrators, had a resounding impact upon higher education. The veterans went to college under a program supported by Public Law 346, the "G.I. Bill." They were something totally new to the "Halls of Ivy," these old-young, war-matured, worldly-wise youths. They were in college to get an education, not just to pass some time pleasantly. Incompetent teachers were not left long in doubt about veterans' evaluations. Professorial rank somehow didn't carry the authority of the military. College teaching has not been the same since.

The termination of the educational benefits for veterans did not shift the focus from quality in college teaching. Student perception of instructors has persisted, and once more students are expressing their desire to rate professors. As students demand their money's worth in effective instruction, it would appear that teaching and teacher preparation are at the beginning of a period of great expectation. But now the nature and conditions of human learning are attracting the attention of some of the nation's leading scholars. Among them are Dressel and Lehmann of Michigan State University, Brunner and Skinner of Harvard University, and McKeachie and Erickson of the University of Michigan. Their findings already point to a more defensible relation of theory to practice, and of content to method. Research on the evaluation of instructional effectiveness is a continuing goal of these few members of the profession. Each year studies relating to the effectiveness or ineffectiveness of various teaching media and the critical factors in successful teaching are begun while others are concluded and published. As a consequence, much more is known now about the subject than was known in 1950. Still more knowledge on which to base the evaluation of instruction and to improve the training of college teachers will soon be available.

Until the present, graduate school faculties have designed and revised their programs in college teaching mainly on the basis of hunches gained largely from personal observation and involvement. Obviously, sound curricular change needs more to guide it than ferment in a faculty or blind decision-making based on subjective opinion.

For the student who can take a planned program of studies terminating with the acquisition of the doctor's degree before beginning a college teaching career, the following blueprint—admittedly traditional in design—is theoretically the appropriate preparation.

General Education Base

Like any other student preparing for a professional calling, one who plans to teach must obtain a broad base of general education. This foundation, upon which all upper-level study is built, should provide a balance between one's cultural heritage and the dynamics of change in society.

For a long time, college faculties have attempted to define the essential elements of a quality program in general education. Current consensus is that general education is not a program of studies that begins with the freshman year and ends abruptly at the completion of the sophomore year. On the contrary, general education is a continuing process.

To a marked degree, the success of a program in general education will depend on the amount of cooperation and rapport developed between the several departments that provide the instruction, between the several discrete disciplines within single departments, and between the professors in broad subject-areas such as the social sciences, the humanities, and the natural sciences.

In the effort to improve general education, there has been a movement toward an interdisciplinary approach to the learnings which all persons need in order to fulfill their responsibilities as citizens. This takes the form of an integrated sequence of required courses. It contrasts sharply with the elective system, in which courses are proliferated and students are encouraged to pick and choose from an array of unrelated offerings and disconnected courses of study.

A sound program of general education embraces the communication skills, including possibly proficiency in a modern language, basic concepts in the natural sciences as well as the social sciences and humanities, and an appreciation of both art and music. In theory, an exposure to this vast body of knowledge should enable a student to identify the universal truths of the society of which he is a part, to make wise decisions, and to realize the need for continued study to meet the demands of life. General education, properly taught, should quicken a student's interest and understanding, whet his appetite for learning, and equip him to play a mature role as a citizen. Thus, while general education has been regarded as the foundation upon which all graduate studies are erected, it is also thought of as the root of a living, fast-growing tree, from which will develop the trunk, the branches and leaves, the blossoms, and, in maturity, the fruit.

Breadth and Depth in Undergraduate Liberal Arts

No four-year program of collegiate study can be designed to include all the courses in arts and sciences necessary to give the learner an awareness of the broad reaches of civilization and human achievement. But for the student who plans to teach, the richer the program of undergraduate studies, the better equipped he will be later to impart knowledge and to assist others to learn. As he gains insight into the humanities, the social sciences, mathematics, and the biological and physical sciences, he should seek opportunities for further penetration into one or more of these areas. He should decide upon a subject field for further concentration.

About midway through his liberal arts program, the student will begin to major in the subject field he may intend to teach. In most colleges, this selection of a major field occurs at the end of the sophomore year. Many colleges also require work in a related field of study, a minor, in order that the combination of a major and a minor will give depth and breadth to a student's liberal studies. Most curricula allow considerable opportunity for elective courses for undergraduates; these should be chosen so as to extend the breadth of the student's contact with subjects outside his major field.

Over the years, academic respectability has developed its own set of standards and ground rules. One must first recognize the fact that the objectives of general education differ completely from those of the disciplines. A student's academic respectability accrues from depth of study in his major field. The student soon learns that it is inappropriate for him to jeopardize his status by departing even temporarily from the traditional mainstream—the disciplinary standards currently in effect. In short, academic respectability means conforming to the rules of his discipline if the student desires to remain in the fold. Pearce's definition of what a discipline is in the modern sense will enable the reader to comprehend what the hall-marks of an educated man are:

> . . . a "discipline" entails ordering, coherence, a sense of relationships—above all a way of knowing and doing something about and with what one knows: not just a command of facts, figures, and the names and numbers of all the players: not something to be given that debilitating name of "content." A "discipline" entails, let us say, a "style," a way of coming to grips with a portion of reality (i.e., "subject-matter") and of sensing its full implications for (ideally) the whole of reality. It entails a theory—which is to say, a generalized conception of such implications. But the theory exists only as it further entails that most practical of activities—living in this world fully, wisely, and well—or at least in the hope of fullness, wisdom, and well-being. . . .
>
> A "discipline" . . . is a "method," but a method for freeing, not capturing, the understanding; moreover, it exists only in inextricable relation to a "content." Thus a content may be taken to be valuable and worthwhile because, by virtue of being what it is, it ramifies into other contents and does not crystallize into something utterly special and specialized. The point is that such freedom and such ramification can be achieved only if the discipline is seen in relation to other disciplines; and the discipline can be seen in relation to other disciplines, only if it is known fully and richly for what it is in itself.[1]

Graduate Study

As a general rule, accredited colleges now insist on at least a year of graduate study as the minimum requirement for anyone being appointed to a regular position on the faculty. There are three kinds of exceptions to this general rule. (1) In fields such as

---

[1] Roy Harvey Pearce, "Education as a Discipline," an address delivered at the Conference of the National Commission on Teacher Education and Professional Standards, National Education Association, Bowling Green State University, Bowling Green, Ohio, June 26, 1958. Used by permission.

art and music, a person with a high native talent, through long years of private study and practice of a kind not leading to an academic degree, may achieve the level of accomplishment and distinction that makes him an artist, entirely worthy of membership in a college faculty. This sort of exception is not as common as it used to be, for programs of instruction in these fields are now widely available in institutions that do grant the usual academic degrees. (2) Another sort of exception is often made for part-time teachers, particularly those who teach a class or two in an evening school or in an extension program. Thus a mature, experienced accountant, probably registered by the state as a Certified Public Accountant, may be entirely acceptable as a teacher of an evening class in the field of accounting. (3) A third sort of exception is commonly made in the large universities, in which graduate students, many of whom are working toward the master's degree, are given appointments as teaching fellows or teaching associates, and are assigned a part-time load of classes, usually at the freshman and sophomore level. The general rule, however, is that, except in the kinds of situations mentioned, all persons who are to be given full-time faculty positions are expected to hold at least the master's degree.

Great weight is given in the selection of faculty members to advanced study beyond the master's degree. The ideal, as indicated earlier, is to fill every teaching position with someone holding the doctor's degree. One who is intending to make a career of college teaching must therefore look toward the graduate school as the door through which he must enter. If he cannot qualify for entrance to the graduate school, he should look for a career in some field other than college teaching.

The possession of an undergraduate degree is often only one of several requirements for admission to graduate study. The student seeking entrance must usually present official transcripts as evidence of having completed a broad and thorough preparation in which he has achieved a better than average academic standing. In addition, the student must have letters of recommendation, affirming his commitment and motivation to pursue graduate work. If he is accepted for entrance to a graduate school, a program of study is built upon his recognized academic interests and abilities, his strengths and weaknesses.

Upon application to the graduate school, a candidate at most universities is subjected to a battery of screening instruments. Among the commonly used standardized tests are the Miller Analogies Test, the Graduate Record Examinations Advanced and Aptitude Tests, the Ohio State Psychological Examination, the Cooperative English Test, and the Watson-Glaser Test of Critical Thinking. Minimum acceptable scores on such tests are sometimes specified. Other measures of selection are undergraduate attainment in a specific area such as modern foreign languages, oral examinations and interviews, character references, and grade-point averages in the bachelor's degree program.

At the doctoral level, selection and retention standards are more restrictive than at the master's level. Selective admission is defended on the ground that the Ph.D. or Ed.D. degrees are the highest awarded. The limited acceptances are made in the belief that the screening processes employed are valid predictors for learning ability and leadership.

Under the prevailing system, graduate study in the United States is specialized education. Quite generally the major emphasis is upon a narrow concentration and research in a subject matter area. In the absence of a common core of content or pattern of preparation for college teaching, the doctoral student usually selects with the advice and approval of his faculty adviser certain advanced courses in order to obtain a satisfactory grasp of his subject major. The attainment of this goal is commonly tested by preliminary or comprehensive examinations, administered toward the end of the prescribed program. If successful, the student prepares a dissertation, with the guidance of his research adviser, in accordance with approved methods of scholarly investigation. This thesis should either contribute to the knowledge of a particular subject or give evidence of professional competence in the solution of a practical problem.

Most students are left largely to their own initiative as they embark on the thesis-writing stage. At some graduate schools, thesis seminars are scheduled in each department. Where thesis guidance is provided under the direction of a graduate student committee or by an adviser, each student is required periodically to render a progress report. Frequently students react to one another's efforts. The seminars afford professors an opportunity to check on the quality of the research in progress, and to stimulate students to complete their dissertations without undue procrastination.

The contacts between the thesis adviser and the graduate student are usually close, but much time may be required before this relationship comes to fruition. A graduate student may spend literally months groping for a vital research topic worthy of acceptance by the faculty as a dissertation problem. Many students complete their course programs and pass their comprehensive examinations, but fail to finish the dissertation. They go through life explaining that, though they do not hold a doctorate, they have fulfilled *all* the requirements *but* the dissertation. Such people are laughingly known in academic circles as A.B.D.'s (All But the Dissertation). People with such qualifications can obtain beginning positions in college teaching, but most soon reach a ceiling beyond which they cannot advance either in academic status or into an institution of higher quality.

The necessity of the thesis requirement and its actual contribution to proficiency in college teaching have been questioned. Some, like Kirk,[2] advocate relegating the dissertation to the status of an exercise in research and essay form. Some, on the other hand, suggest devoting more time and professorial attention to dissertation preparation, even at the cost of credit hours in regular courses. Others advocate utilizing the efforts and abilities of graduate students through the award of more research contracts to graduate schools by federal agencies such as the National Institute of Mental Health, the Atomic Energy Commission, the National Science Foundation, the Agency for International Development, and the National Aeronautics and Space Administration.

At the end of the graduate program, the student is expected to qualify for the degree by a final examination, usually oral but sometimes both written and oral. The final examination tests the candidate's intellectual abilities and his knowledge of his special field of subject matter and allied fields, and usually there is a rather intensive period of interrogation over the candidate's dissertation. Commonly there is a requirement also that the dissertation must be bound or made generally available in some acceptable form. The dissertation produced by the candidate for a graduate

---

[2] Grayson L. Kirk, "Speed Up of the Ph.D. Degree," *School and Society* (January 31, 1959).

degree bears witness to the caliber of the institution as well as of the student who wrote it.

The Basic Professional Preparation

In the past college teachers have generally entered on their careers with no professional preparation for teaching at the college level, and without any special introduction to the other responsibilities customarily carried by faculty members. Some, indeed, have had preparation for and experience in teaching at the elementary or secondary levels of the public schools, prior to their entrance to college teaching. The extent to which such preparation and experience carry over into the college level of teaching has never been determined. In practice, prior experience in teaching at the elementary or secondary school level seems to be largely discounted in evaluating the qualifications of a candidate for a teaching position in a college or university. In junior colleges, however, experience as a high school teacher seems to be definitely advantageous. Also it is common to insist on some teaching experience at the elementary or secondary level for those appointed to positions in departments or schools of education in colleges and universities.

From the point of view of those who prepare college teachers, the assumption has long been that, by a heavy concentration in the subject matter of his teaching subject, plus a research experience gained by preparing a dissertation, any person would be adequately qualified professionally for service as a college or university faculty member. Specific professional preparation, now universally required of teachers in American elementary and secondary schools, has never seemed to be necessary or even desirable for college teachers, at least from the point of view of those who control the policies of the graduate schools in the United States.

Although professional preparation has not been a part of the required program leading to college teaching, most graduate students do get some opportunity during their years of advanced study to serve as graduate assistants, or teaching associates or fellows, and in that capacity they may teach some classes. In most universities the graduate students are looked upon as a source of cheap labor to teach a large part of freshman and sophomore classes rather inexpensively. Graduate students thus have an opportunity to find out whether they like to teach, and possibly to get some little intimation about their success as teachers. Rarely does the department or graduate school take interest in making this service a genuinely professional experience—one in which, through adequate supervision and guidance, teaching techniques could be improved and the teaching associate or fellow given an insight into the varied nature of faculty responsibilities beyond those of classroom teaching.

Although the characteristic attitude of graduate schools toward professional preparation for college teaching is one of indifference, almost disdain, there are some signs of a change. To prepare scholars who are also teachers, some graduate schools, especially of late, have made provisions for professional preparation. The content of the professional education sequence varies with each institution. The instruction in college teaching may be given either by means of a regularly scheduled non-credit seminar attended by potential college teachers from all disciplines, or by means of a course within each department. These courses usually give attention to ideas for instruction in classroom procedures, techniques of teaching, testing and evaluation, and teaching problems.

At a few graduate centers, students planning to go into college teaching are given opportunities to explore different and better techniques of teaching. This is accomplished in a variety of ways. At one institution it may be through the appointment of teaching fellows, who work directly under the supervision of a senior professor in their discipline. Here the teaching fellow has major responsibility for conducting discussion sessions in a regular lecture course. He may be asked to attend a departmental practicum, in which other teaching fellows analyze problems and discuss techniques for their own improvement. The "Graduate School 701" at Ohio State University, an optional course concerned with problems of teaching, is probably unique. Here students from seventy-five graduate departments of the university, mostly teaching assistants, convene regularly to hear guest lecturers and participate in open forum discussions.[3]

A small number of graduate schools have established a core of courses in higher education and in professional education, usually

---

[3] Everett Walters, "A Course on College Teaching," *School and Society* (October 5, 1963), pp. 286–287.

supplementary to the general academic requirements for an advanced degree. These are offered to those who declare an intention to teach, and at a few institutions are reinforced by opportunities for students to teach one or two courses under faculty supervision, either during or at the close of their doctoral programs of study.

Donovan[4] polled some 77 multi-purpose institutions of higher education, asking whether they offered doctoral programs with a major in higher education for the purpose of preparing students for teaching, administration, or research at that level. Nineteen reported that they did. Those who responded to a further request for titles and course descriptions indicated that most of these offerings are concerned with teaching in higher education, and with college or university organization, administration, and personnel.

Courses in college teaching are proliferating along with those in other disciplines, but little else of significance has been done to guarantee a flow of new college teachers who are both academically and professionally well educated. A national survey of programs and courses on higher education has reported the growth of professional education courses and internships, but no attempt was made in the survey to determine the quality of these offerings. The small beginning that has been made toward the inclusion of professional courses on higher education in the graduate programs of some universities bodes well.

> Nothing in recent years has done more for the quality of education in this country than the development of a large interest in the content of education at every level by scholars and scientists of the highest competence and achievement. Quite certainly we cannot be satisfied in the future with the artificial split that has sometimes obtained in the past between so-called methodologists and subject-matter specialists.[5]

Graduate programs with a major in higher education and the offering of courses on college teaching represent well directed effort, but none of these efforts is sufficient by itself, and collectively

---

[4] George F. Donovan (director), *A Study of Doctoral Programs with a Major in Higher Education in United States Universities,* a report prepared by the class members in Ed. 651 (Washington: Catholic University of America, Graduate School of Arts and Sciences, 1963), p. 4.

[5] Sterling M. McMurrin, "The Teacher and His Education for a Free Society," *Foundations for Excellence,* The fifteenth yearbook of the American Association of Colleges for Teacher Education (Washington: the Association, 1962), p. 34.

they fall far short of meeting the acute national need for college teachers and administrators. It is not enough that students be given a few courses on the status of higher education in America, an "audition" in the form of an opportunity to teach a course, and then be told to stay or go. They are needed too badly for such profligate waste. When a student has reached the end of his graduate school program at a reputable institution, his very presence there bears testimony to his academic, intellectual, and personal qualifications and interest. It is a reflection on the quality of the program of professional preparation offered him if he cannot perform creditably in the classroom, especially when he has demonstrated his motivation to teach by his acceptance and election of the program.

Spectacular technological and scientific developments seem actually to be hastening the ultimate marriage of the subject-oriented part of the program with an interest in the theory and practice of teaching. This union is both necessary and convenient. Graduate school faculties, however, except in rare instances, still attempt to resolve their own problems and implement ways to improve teaching each in their own way, usually ignoring the potential contributions of on-campus schools of education.

Each year brings new hope of a dramatic breakthrough. Currently, the desire of leading scholars to perform their responsibilities creditably and efficiently has brought a renewed interest in teaching. The cultivation of the skills required to perform brilliantly in the classroom are viewed on most campuses as both an in-service and a pre-service responsibility.

The effect has been to make college teachers in training aware that they may be expected to continue their preparation through and beyond their graduate studies. Tomorrow, hopefully, a fully coordinated program of academic and professional studies might well be standard preparation for college teachers.

The Internship

It is to the advantage of both beginning teacher and his college that the initial experiences in the field prove satisfactory. Having taken the pains to screen a candidate whose qualifications appear superior, an institution cannot afford to lose him, when circumstances quite beyond his control, but not beyond the control of the institution, subsequently cause field supervisors to judge him unfit. Neither can the beginning teacher afford to fail in his first assignment. Therefore it behooves both the beginner and his mature faculty colleagues to anticipate and to eliminate as many as possible of the factors that might contribute to failure.

In many of the learned professions one who has completed his academic preparation is expected or required to undergo a period of internship before he is considered fully competent to assume professional responsibilities in an unsupervised situation. The academic internship is essentially a period of supervised practice, during which the beginner performs professional duties under the watchful eye of a mature and competent practitioner. The practice under supervision builds up the beginner's confidence in his own competence, for his own ideas of the way to carry out his new professional duties are reinforced by the approval of his supervisor, and a mistake, if the beginner should make one, is very likely to be caught and corrected before any damage is done. There is every reason to believe that a period of internship would be highly beneficial to the great majority of those who expect to enter the college teaching profession.

The internship is neither the time nor place to teach learning theory. It is however the place to learn how one applies basic principles to classroom procedures.

The scope and unpredictable character of his initial assignment can do much to prejudice a beginning intern's chances of success or failure. If the experience is to be successful, both the intern and his faculty supervisor must gauge the realities carefully. The teaching load also must be weighed against the amount of preparation it will necessitate and against the intern's other commitments, such as: (1) the services (if any) he is expected to render in his capacity as an assistant or fellow or scholarship holder; (2) the demands of his graduate studies; (3) the special scholarly activities or research for which he may appear to have special aptitude and upon which the institution wishes to capitalize; and (4) the committee, guidance, and social activities which will be required of him. Achieving an effective balance between these activities is possible only if they are assigned relative values and so weighted by a unanimous faculty and their chairmen.

Frequently college teachers are asked to "fill in" on courses which are not within their particular areas of competency. Since prescriptive measures are being discussed, it must be noted that this is not recommended for neophytes. Beginners need the self-confidence that accompanies familiarity with course content; they can ill afford the additional time consumed by superficial preparation in an alien field. For the same reason, each intern should be apprised of his teaching assignment a month or more in advance of the semester.

The proper atmosphere between neophyte teachers and their department chairmen should be one of collaboration focused on the task at hand, rather than "snoopervision." This strengthens the intern's self-reliance, minimizes debilitating tensions, and makes the task of guidance easier, as young interns more readily initiate discussions of problems which they are encountering. Such discussions with department chairmen, who cannot audit their courses, are a major index of an intern's adjustment.

Seminars in which beginning college teachers have an opportunity to discuss problems with their fellows render considerable support and aid. This is especially so where senior faculty members are generous enough to contribute their own knowledge and experience in their capacities as subject matter advisers.

Since all efforts must be evaluated sooner or later, department chairmen and beginning teachers should reach some degree of unanimity early as to the criteria, evidence, and scale to be applied. This is true both in the case of teachers' evaluations of students and chairmen's evaluation of teachers. Unless the criteria, evidence, and scale are clearly identified, prescribed, and delimited, the evaluative process becomes a matter of subjective impressions and opinions, often incorrect and seldom supportable.

CHAPTER V

Conditions of Service

There are many sources of college teachers; not all come to faculty appointments via the liberal arts colleges and graduate schools. They are not "born" teachers and, despite special curricula designed to prepare them, relatively few are "bred." In most instances they are recruited.

The teacher with the reputation as an outstanding scholar in his field is readily identified. Institutions with policies of continuous recruitment to replace retiring faculty members seek persons of this caliber and negotiate directly to attract them to their faculties.

Individuals who are active in professional organizations and regional educational activities, especially those whose work is subsequently published, establish personal contacts and reputations. Such participation often enables appointing authorities to identify potential recruits.

The graduate schools are traditionally a rich source of prospective teachers. As noted earlier, almost half of those recruited as new teachers are taken directly from the graduate schools. The recommendations of graduate school faculty members, especially those acting as sponsors of doctoral candidates, influence those recruiting college teachers. The aversion to "in-breeding" has given impetus to the custom of informal intercollege communication for placement of graduates.

Most degree-granting institutions operate student placement services which attempt to inform students and alumni of positions which are available and suitable to their talents. Students wishing to teach should register with their college placement office.

Candidates are seldom selected on the basis of an unsolicited application submitted to the college of their choice. More receptive of unsolicited applications are the agencies for foreign service such as UNESCO'S International Association of Universities or the Office of Education's Educational Missions Branch.

Less fruitful avenues of employment include the United States

Employment Services, commercial teachers' agencies, the "Teachers Available" rosters of various professional publications, such as the AAUP Bulletin.

Having identified prospective candidates, the institution faces the task of screening them. Screening attempts to predict an individual's probable performance in relation to the needs of the employing institution. Ideally, these needs take the form of criteria by which the applicant is measured.

The nature of the criteria varies according to the location, philosophy, purpose, control, and tradition of the institution involved, and reflects the autonomy and diversity of American colleges and universities. The criteria most commonly applied by four-year institutions are academic scholarship, professional achievement, and research accomplishments. Increasingly, leadership and service in the vast and urgent educational enterprise are also being considered.

In general, community colleges stress effective classroom teaching above all other qualifications. The prime consideration for a person's selection and retention, therefore, rests upon competency in teaching and in assisting students through sympathetic counseling and clarifying operations. Frequently, in states where public community colleges are legally an extension of the secondary school, a prescribed program of preparation leading to teacher certification is mandated by the state board of education for appointments to teach in grades 13 and 14. Other states require a master's degree, one or more theoretical courses in education, and an internship.

Evidence of a candidate's qualifications is usually evaluated by a faculty committee, the appropriate department head, dean, president of the institution, and board of trustees—by any or all of these, and probably in this order. His credentials take many forms. Quality of scholarship is indicated by the candidate's earned degrees, the transcript of his academic record, the honors awarded him, his letters of recommendation, and his published writings and research. Professional attitudes and ethics may be attested to by former associates and colleagues. Not uncommonly, doctoral sponsors receive long distance telephone calls about candidates' potential. These unofficial appraisals may carry considerably more weight with employment authorities than formal letters of recommendation, of which experienced administrators take a rather dim view.

Responses by 577 member institutions in the American Association of Colleges for Teacher Education pointed out the following weaknesses in letters of recommendation: a) vagueness about the individual's service as a member of the university community, the quality of his research and publications, his role in professional societies, his community service; and b) inaccurate assessment of personality by unqualified respondents.[1]

The candidate's appearance, personality, habits, pursuits, associates, social and professional affiliations, and civic contributions are part of the evidence. His preparation and prior performance in teaching are being given increasing consideration by college and university administrators.

Colleges and universities offer many attractions to potential faculty members. Among them are personnel policies which under present tax laws are more enticing than salary rewards to an increasing number of "name" professors. Others include generous institution-financed housing loans; travel budgets; guaranteed research support both in terms of recurring funds and light teaching assignments; a climate of democratic administrative controls in matters affecting institutional policy and personnel; adequate teaching and secretarial assistance; strong financial support for participation in professional activities at local and national levels; and ample benefits under the salary schedule for pension and annuity.

Even more common benefits are low rentals in institution-owned housing, leased land for home building, reduced or free tuition for children, free or low cost medical and surgical care, group life and major medical insurance plans, permanent disability income insurance programs, sabbaticals, and special grants for advanced study at foreign institutions. Faculty members whose duties require them to live on campus may be offered free room and board.

When a candidate has been recommended for appointment, he is informed usually by the dean of the college appointing him of the conditions of employment. Instructors generally are appointed

---

[1] Herbert R. Schueler, "Recruitment and Appointment of Faculty," in *Improvement of Instruction in Higher Education,* a report prepared by the Subcommittee on Improvement of Instruction of the Committee on Studies, Study Series No. 6 (Washington: The American Association of Colleges for Teacher Education, 1962), pp. 23–29.

on an annual basis. Seldom at this rank do instructors receive more than three one-year appointments, after which they are either promoted or not retained on the faculty.

Assistant professors in many institutions must have the earned doctorate or present evidence of being in the thesis stage of their doctoral program. Initial appointment is usually for a term of three years. Many institutions permit assistant professors to have a second three-year term at the expiration of which they are expected to move forward to the next higher rank. If retained beyond six years' service at the rank of assistant professor, they receive in some colleges and universities that rank without limitation of term. In other institutions, one who has held an assistant professorship for the maximum term, and is not deemed worthy of promotion, is not retained on the faculty. At the end of any year an assistant professor, who has met the qualifications for promotion, may be advanced to an associate professorship.

Associate and full professors usually enjoy tenure and may not be removed except for cause. In some instances, the term of office is indefinite and at the pleasure of the board of control.

A faculty member may be appointed on the academic year or calendar year basis. If the former, his teaching program is for both fall and spring semesters or for three quarters of the four quarter schedule. During these periods he is expected to instruct the courses assigned and to be available for related duties. A faculty member appointed for the calendar year is usually eligible for one month's vacation. Otherwise, he is expected to devote the remainder of the time to his assigned duties, usually on-campus.

Each newly appointed or reappointed faculty member receives a communication from the appropriate college or university authority setting forth the exact nature and terms of his appointment. Conditions vary as to procedures beyond the first year.

Promotional Policies and Practices

Unlike their counterparts at lower levels of education, the faculties of institutions of higher education are distinguished by academic rank, which carries several implications. As an instructor, the college teacher is a newcomer, unproven, inexperienced, and on trial. His appointment may or may not be renewed the following year. His orientation to his task, the students, and the University, is largely unformulated. His role may not be the one to which he aspires, that is, he may be assigned to teach undergraduate courses, though he prefers to do research. He will be observed by his colleagues and administrators for evidence of the "scholarly activity, teaching effectiveness, research accomplishments, competence, experience, and general usefulness to the institution"[2] which usually comprise the criteria for promotion.

As already stated, to be reappointed, instructors quite universally must also demonstrate progress in the pursuit of an earned graduate degree. Generally, instructors are limited to a maximum of two or three one-year reappointments, after which, failing to gain the assistant professorial rank, they are dropped.

An assistant professorship places no less of a burden of proof upon the individual than an instructorship does, in terms of his continuing scholarship, teaching efficiency, productive research, and candidacy for the associate rank. In some institutions an assistant professor appointed for a third three-year term automatically is given tenure. Most college teachers do not desire to be "frozen" with little hope of promotion and at so limited a salary.

Despite increasing numbers entering college teaching without the doctoral degree, most institutions make the degree a mandatory requirement for associate or full professorship. Among other criteria is the individual's capacity as a teacher—important although somewhat difficult to assess. Interestingly, studies have shown outstanding teaching to be a powerful factor among promotion criteria. Byrnes and Jamrich found it to be such in 51.9 per cent of the institutions they surveyed.[3] Logan Wilson cites a survey of 71 member institutions of the Association of State Universities and Land Grant Colleges, two-thirds of which approve the promotion of superior teachers who may or may not be productive researchers.[4] Despite this, the classroom of the college teacher has, in most

---

2 Provost's Cabinet, *Policy with Respect to Academic Promotions* (New Brunswick: Rutgers University, 1954), p. 1.

3 Francis C. Byrnes and John X. Jamrich, "Survey of Policies and Practices Relating to Improved Instruction," *Improvement of Instruction in Higher Education,* a report prepared by the Subcommittee on Improvement of Instruction of the Committee on Studies, Study Series No. 6 (Washington: The American Association of Colleges for Teacher Education, 1962), pp. 19–22.

4 Address by Dr. Logan Wilson, President, American Council on Education, at the Diamond Anniversary Convention, Association of State Universities and Land Grant Colleges, Washington, November 11–14, 1962.

institutions, remained sacrosanct, exempt from appraisal by anyone other than students. Evaluation of college teaching, therefore, is less than an objective procedure, which may explain why the more readily observable doctoral degrees, scholarship, research, and publication continue to be the major criteria for admission to the associate professorial rank. Unfortunately, research and publication are too frequently assessed in terms of volume rather than content.

Sometimes fully eligible persons are not promoted primarily because of the lack of openings at higher ranks, or because of insufficient funds assigned to departments in a new operating budget. This condition is less frequent today than formerly, when arbitrary limitations were in vogue specifying the number or percentage in each rank, or when operating income, legislative appropriations, and grants were more difficult to obtain. Qualified faculty members are in greater demand today and distinguished service professors are sought after by the best institutions. This caliber of person is able today to name the conditions of his employment.

In most four-year institutions, faculty members having earned doctor's degrees may expect to become associate professors in about five years—longer perhaps in a complex, multi-purpose institution where rank is harder to achieve. Promotions are usually more rapid in smaller institutions, where rank often carries a less attractive salary.

Opportunities for promotion are engendered by (a) retirements or deaths of senior faculty members, (b) proselyting of top faculty by other institutions, and (c) departmental expansions.

Administrators are understandably cautious about awarding associate professor appointments, since the rank usually carries tenure. While excellent college teachers may never exceed this rank and yet remain excellent, the security of the position sometimes makes it difficult to resist the temptation to relax.

Ordinarily, tenure status is a privilege accorded to those who, after a long trial, prove worthy of membership on the permanent faculty. The college or university provides the scholar a platform from which he can be heard. Should his ideas or proposals be unpopular, radical, or unorthodox, he might be suspect and his academic freedom could be in jeopardy. Tenure safeguards him against unwarranted attack from without or within the academy, and is necessary to insure uninterrupted intellectual ferment in a faculty.

Professional associations, such as the American Association of University Professors and regional accrediting agencies, recommend that faculty members participate in the formulation of criteria for tenure and advancement, so that faculty personnel policies may represent consensus of the instructional staff in a college or university, and so have a positive effect even upon "sluggards."[5]

Full professorial rank is normally the highest recognition an institution can bestow on members of its faculty. It is not or should not be an acknowledgment of seniority. It attests to the superior quality of its holder—academically, intellectually, and personally —and implies responsibilities as well as privileges. In the stronger universities and colleges, the rank of full professor is usually given only to those who enjoy a scholarly reputation among colleagues in their own field of specialization outside the local institution.

Some leading universities and colleges have instituted a superior academic rank, above that of full professor, sometimes designated "distinguished service professor." This is normally reserved for a very few faculty members who have brought great distinction to the institution by their scholarly activities. The distinguished service professor receives a salary well beyond the top of the regular faculty scale. Quite commonly he holds a "named" professorship, that is, one designated by the name of a donor who has provided the funds that enable the paying of an unusual salary.

In some cases the faculty member's duties involve some administrative responsibilities, which he may find onerous or not, according to his bent. Some 10 to 15 per cent of faculty positions combine administrative service, so one can aspire to such positions with reasonable optimism, should one be so inclined. These administrative assignments are usually open to all ranks of assistant professor and above, but most frequently are held by those in the higher academic ranks.

Assuring the continuing professional growth of staff members is an ever-present challenge and responsibility confronting admin-

[5] Commission on Institutions of Higher Education, *The Conditions and Responsibilities of Employment in Higher Education,* Proceedings of the 72nd Annual Convention of the Middle States Association of Colleges and Secondary Schools (New York: the Association, 1958), p. 71.

istrative officials in institutions of higher education. Affording public and financial recognition of achievement and merit, awarding grants, fellowships, and scholarships, regulating salary increases and tenure criteria on bases of achievement and contribution, adjusting teaching loads and schedules to accommodate research enterprises, allocating funds and time to subsidize attendance at professional conferences, and finding ways to reward creative individuals who warrant recognition—these are but some of the more positive tasks of the administrator. The way in which young college teachers involve themselves in all phases of academic life is an index of their eligibility for higher ranks. The readiness and effectiveness young college teachers bring to such administrative responsibilities is an index of their eligibility for higher ranks, and the manner in which members of these higher ranks execute these tasks attests to both their own professional adequacy and the effectiveness of the over-all development program initiated by the institution.

Institutional and Faculty Organization

So complex is the organization of modern institutions of higher education that the beginning college teacher may suspect that there is no organization at all, but rather an aggregation of discrete units (departments, divisions, schools, colleges, and institutes), the inhabitants of which are largely oblivious of each other's existence. In some institutions this suspicion is substantiated by a breakdown in administrative communication, so that the members of separate departments become divorced from the over-all institutional effort and, as a result, substitute their own interests for those of the institution as a whole. Most institutions, however, conform to a general organizational pattern. The following pattern, not without variation, is discernible at many colleges and universities.

The ultimate authority in an institution resides in its governing board, known variously as board of trustees, board of regents, board of visitors, etc. In privately controlled institutions, membership on the governing board may be self-perpetuating, or the members may be appointed by the church body with which the college is affiliated, or some members may be elected by the alumni. In state-controlled institutions the members of the governing boards are usually appointed by the governor of the state, commonly with the advice and consent of one or both houses of the legislature.[6]

If the board has a large membership, its most immediate liaison with the college or university may be through its executive committee. Commonly someone on the staff of the institution is appointed to serve as secretary to the board, with responsibility for keeping a record of the board's proceedings.

The board appoints the institution's president, who is accountable to the board as its chief executive officer.[7] The president's main function is to coordinate the educational aspirations of the institution with its physical and fiscal realities. His usual problems may be characterized as "proliferation": of students, courses, programs, staff, equipment, facilities, expenses—of everything except, probably, an adequacy of support. A second major presidential function stems from the last mentioned element: fund raising.

Because it is beyond the ability of a single man to function effectively in all the areas implied in the educational, personal, physical, and fiscal dimensions of an institution, certain responsibilities and authority must be delegated. Usually four or more major officials assist the president directly; often they bear the title of vice-president. One will be the academic vice-president, sometimes known as provost or dean of faculties. Another will be the chief business officer or treasurer. Quite generally the public relations function, including fund raising, will be assigned another official with vice-presidential status. Except in the smaller colleges, the official in charge of student personnel services will also rank as one of the major administrative officers.

The college or university president, even as the President of the United States, may be assisted in the formulation of administrative policy by a cabinet or administrative committee, consisting of the major officers such as the vice-presidents, the college or university secretary, the registrar, the director of admissions, and directors of separate divisions such as extension or alumni affairs.

Since 1940, new areas of knowledge, with their accompanying disciplines, programs, and courses, have increased the lower ech-

---

[6] S. V. Martorana, *College Boards of Trustees* (New York: The Center for Applied Research in Education, Inc., 1963).

[7] Ralph Prator, *The College President* (New York: The Center for Applied Research in Education, Inc., 1963), p. 37.

elon administrative positions. Assisting the academic vice-president or provost in his task of administering the educational efforts of the institution are the deans (of colleges, professional schools, extension division); the directors (of development, personnel, admissions, institutional research, audio-visual services, summer session, placement, public relations, and athletics); the librarian; and the alumni secretary.

To the treasurer, or vice-president for business affairs, falls the task of administering the financial operations of the institution. Aspects of the business organization of any college or university include: (1) budget, (2) accounting, (3) cashier, (4) non-academic personnel, (5) purchasing, (6) dormitories and housing, and (7) physical plant operation and maintenance.[8] Assisting the chief financial officer in his task are such persons as the bursar, bookstore manager, internal auditor, research contract officer, investment counsel, cost study director, and systems and methods coordinator. The range of titles evidences the broad scope of the business organization's operations. Without the business organization, the academic operations would be unworkable; and without the academic organization, the business office would have no reason for existence. The efforts of these two administrative areas must be intimately coordinated by the president.

Student affairs are another broad area of institutional administration. This area includes all aspects of student life on the campus other than classroom instruction and the student's immediate academic interests. Under a major official, sometimes known as dean of students or director of student personnel services, are organized such functions as pre-college guidance, admissions (sometimes this function is placed under the academic vice-president), orientation of new students, counseling of students, student health service, placement service, student discipline, financial assistance to students, the non-business aspects of student feeding and housing, and student organizations and activities. This area of service is being given increasing emphasis in American institutions of higher education. Faculty members often have opportunity to serve in some of the student personnel functions, such as counseling, or

---

8 Kenneth Erfft, "The Vice-President for Business Affairs," in *Administrators in Higher Education: Their Functions and Coordination,* Gerald P. Burns (ed.) (New York: Harper & Row, Publishers, Inc., 1962), pp. 125–140.

sponsorship of student organizations, or in the orientation procedures.

The prospective college teacher may need to be oriented to his own role within the somewhat complicated pattern of college and university organization. As a member of its teaching staff, he is part of the organization's broadest base. He is a member of a department, and of a school or college which may be part of a university. He is thus accountable to a department chairman who is, in turn, accountable to a dean who may be accountable to the academic vice-president or to the president of the institution.

Though it may seem that the college teacher is the unenviable "low man on the totem pole," it must be noted that faculty members are typically organized as a legislative body. As such, they collectively exercise an important influence or control over the academic policies and practices of the college or university. Furthermore, faculty members as individuals, through participating in interdepartmental and institution-wide committees or institutes, are exercising increasing influence upon the policies and practices of the institutions which employ them. Appointment, promotion, salaries, and tenure, traditionally an administrative province, now often come under the purview of faculty committees, of departmental sections, of a representative faculty body sometimes known as the senate, or of the entire faculty as a legislative body. Similarly, problems of curricula, student personnel services, intramural and interscholastic athletics, public relations, and institutional expansion are discussed, and policy recommendations are formulated, via faculty conferences. Thus, faculty committees or conferences serve to broaden the teacher's acquaintance with the rest of the organization, and deepen his perspective as to the goals, philosophy, and function of the institution as a whole.

At large institutions with thousands of students, the need for representative government for faculty members becomes more evident. It is simply impractical to solve a problem by calling a general meeting involving several hundred, or perhaps even a few thousand, people. A more practical expedient is the faculty "senate," a legislative body, with its criteria for membership, its ratios of representation, and its specific functions varying from institution to institution. But as an academic agency the faculty senate has not been an unqualified success. Oliver Carmichael attributes most of the problem to a lack of provision for realistic and systematic attention to broad educational programs, policies, and practices.[9] He suggests that the membership ought to include representatives of the governing board and administration, so the agency can effectively initiate basic changes in policies and practice.[10]

Effective Utilization of Faculty Resources

American colleges and universities, sadly aware of the inadequacy of supporting funds and the shortage of well qualified scholars for teaching positions, are under pressure to derive the maximum output from their present faculty. Administrators and faculty now recognize hitherto unnoticed ways of exploiting the time of professional staff members and previously ignored methods of utilizing effectively the time and effort of master teachers.

Because an individual's sense of adequacy, "belonging," contribution, and acceptance can either minimize the impact of heavy schedules or render them unbearable, many efforts are directed toward improving teacher morale. As more than a few studies have indicated, this takes more than an increase in salary.

College teachers are a mobile group, responsive to job opportunities in other communities, and singularly adaptable. But to adapt simultaneously to a new social milieu and a new professional climate takes time which institutions can ill afford. Unassisted by an institutional effort at orientation, the newcomers may suffer such demoralizing frustration and anxiety as to negate their effectiveness entirely during this period.

Orientation of new faculty members has been the subject of several articles and studies during the past few years, attesting to increasing administrative interest.[11] There is a trend toward welcoming incoming faculty members socially; apprising them of available housing accommodations; inducting their wives into "Newcomers"

---

[9] Oliver C. Carmichael, *Universities: Commonwealth and American* (New York: Harper & Row, Publishers, Inc., 1959), pp. 105–106.

[10] Gerald P. Burns (ed.), *Administrators in Higher Education* (New York: Harper & Row, Publishers, Inc., 1961), p. 76.

[11] Harold E. Hyde, "Orienting New Faculty," *Improvement of Instruction in Higher Education,* a report prepared by the Subcommittee on Improvement of Instruction of the Committee on Studies, Study Series No. 6 (Washington: The American Association of Colleges for Teacher Education, 1962), pp. 31–47.

clubs; inviting them to social events such as teas, receptions, and dinners; inducting them into faculty clubs; and introducing them to local stores, banks, and churches. All this is best done by visits to the campus and its environs prior to appointment. Some colleges mail printed materials, including information on retirement, insurance, hospitalization, sample forms, personnel policy statements, curriculum guides, and local and campus newspapers to incoming faculty members.

Stripling developed in detail the following promising approaches to the professional orientation of new college teachers:[12]

1. arrangement for new faculty members to report for work at least two weeks before classes begin;
2. orientation conferences;
3. assignment of new faculty members to experienced faculty members;
4. light teaching loads for the initial semester;
5. conferences with key administrative officials;
6. observation of registration and counseling procedures;
7. introduction to students at student receptions;
8. use of charts, film, slides, and other visual aids describing the institution and its functions; and
9. assignment to committees.

Hyde focused attention upon modern methods being used for staff orientation[13] and the procedures 247 institutions had used in evaluating their programs for orienting new staff. The survey reported that such methods as the friendly faculty mentor, structured pre-college opening programs, and planned series of meetings proved worth the effort involved.

Realizing that knowledge of subject matter and skill in communicating it effectively to students are not necessarily related, institutions of higher education are preparing their faculty personnel to be efficient and effective teachers. Many are operating in-service programs, designed to clarify the teaching task within the context of the requirements and problems peculiar to the employing institutions, utilizing seminars, staff meetings, and papers concerned with problems and methods of teaching.

---

[12] Robert O. Stripling, "Orientation Practices for New College Faculty Members," AAUP *Bulletin*, Vol. XL, No. 4 (December 1954), pp. 555–562.

[13] Hyde, p. 32.

The tasks of teachers have been studied to identify those which are extraneous. Consequently, committee obligations and unimportant speaking engagements have been reduced to a minimum in many instances. Secretarial and clerical help, graduate assistants, and IBM computers have significantly reduced the number of routine tasks that previously accounted for large blocks of the teacher's time, thus freeing him for his professional functions.

The curriculum has been scrutinized in the effort to capitalize on the present faculty. Overlapping or repetitive courses, those of marginal importance to the program, and poorly patronized courses have been ruthlessly pruned.

There has been a resurgence of interest in independent study which places the responsibility for learning squarely upon the student. Advocates of independent study believe that, while it demands considerable knowledge and skill of the teacher, as well as detailed preparation in its initial stages, it produces dividends in the scholarly maturation of students and affords the teacher more time in the long run for preparation of the formal presentation for which he is responsible.

To expand the impact of superior teachers, some colleges have allowed professors to lecture at other institutions. This has eased the problem of smaller institutions faced with the impossibility of obtaining outstanding authorities on a full-time basis, and it has injected vigor into their departmental discussions; but it creates problems bearing upon institutional accreditation and service loads of instructors.

Team teaching programs have been initiated, affording faculty members opportunities to prepare intensively in their areas of special interest for presentation to large groups of students. Other advantages of such programs are:

1. In-service education of teachers through frequent team meetings;
2. Ability to vary group size appropriately when necessary for instructional purposes;
3. Ability to regroup students frequently according to achievement, ability, and interest levels;
4. Ability to exchange teachers, affording opportunities to exploit their special talents, knowledge, and training;
5. Improved guidance of students through teachers' exchange of information and spirit of fellowship; and

6. Improved correlation of subject matter through cooperative planning.[14]

The service of valuable staff members has been lengthened through extension of the normal, mandatory retirement age or re-employment on a year-to-year, untenured basis beyond it.

Television, films, tape recordings, teaching machines, and pro-grammed learning can and are being used effectively to apply and extend teaching talent, although resistance to their use is still strong. Where used, daily observation and evaluation assess their potential applicability and effectiveness. Such teaching devices lend themselves to the presentation of particular kinds of material in certain circumstances, the problems being the definition of these materials and circumstances.

Evaluating Effectiveness of Teaching

Despite the pages in professional publications devoted to its discussion, "teaching effectiveness" remains poorly defined. The evaluators of teacher effectiveness are many: administrators, de-partment chairmen, deans, colleagues, students, and, less inti-mately, parents. Studies have indicated that persons in these cate-gories may equate "good" or "effective" teaching with quite dis-similar characteristics. Colleagues tend to equate good teaching with creativeness, while students equate it with personality.[15] This is not surprising when one considers the vantage point from which these appraisals are made.

In the prolonged day-to-day conduct of his classes, the teacher's personality projects itself impressively upon his students. If one defines effectiveness narrowly as an ability to communicate his message understandably to the students, then students' appraisals and reactions to a teacher's personality, which operate to facilitate or block that communication, bear considerable relationship to the teacher's effectiveness.

---

14 John A. Brownell (ed.), *Second Annual Report to the Ford Foundation,* by the Claremont Teaching Team Program, Claremont Graduate School, Claremont, California, 1960–61, pp. 2–3.

15 Winslow R. Hatch (ed.), *Special Reports: Clearinghouse of Studies on Higher Education,* Special Report No. 2, U.S. Department of Health, Education, and Wel-fare, Office of Education, Circular No. 563 (Washington: U.S. Government Print-ing Office, 1959), pp. 4–12.

If one holds a broader definition of effectiveness, including learning and retention of knowledge, students' appraisals may lose their validity. In the study last cited, it was noted that the data did not support the hypothesis that students in classes of teachers receiving high student effectiveness ratings would learn more than those with teachers rated ineffective.[16]

If the criterion of continuing student interest is applied as an index of teacher effectiveness, the data again did "not indicate a very consistent relationship between student ratings and student interest as evidenced by election of advanced courses."[17]

Although the studies that have been made do not support the use of student ratings for the administrative evaluation of the college teacher's effectiveness, the teacher himself may find helpful criticism from the use of one or more of the available scales for student ratings of college teachers. The teacher may find, for example, that his students, when offered the opportunity through use of an evaluation instrument, will indicate that he fails to pay attention to the heating and ventilation of the classroom, or that he speaks in a voice that is not easily audible to many in the class, or that he has one or more personal mannerisms or habits that affect students adversely when he is before the class. Shortcomings such as these should be corrected before they mature into habits. The beginning teacher may find the use of a rating scale by students in his classes of considerable assistance as he attempts to develop his own teaching methods and classroom behavior patterns.

The doubtful validity of student ratings necessitates the use of other agencies of evaluation, such as the instructional and administrative staffs, visiting teams of outstanding teachers, scholars, and administrators such as comprise those of the regional accrediting agencies, and the teachers themselves. The evaluative approach of these groups usually takes two directions: 1) observation of the teacher's performance in relation to various criteria presumed to be conducive to effectiveness; and 2) observation and evaluation of the outcomes of the teaching performance.

Before examining these in greater detail, the reader should recognize some operational definitions. "Teaching effectiveness" is taken to mean the efficacy with which teachers implement the

---

[16] *Ibid.*, p. 11.
[17] *Ibid.*, p. 7.

learning of the students; "learning" is defined as change and growth. By "criteria presumed to be conducive to effectiveness" is meant a series of criteria which have been demonstrated to be both valid and reliable.

The evaluator observes 1) the college teacher's appearance, voice, gestures, and overt attitudes; 2) choice and variation of presentation method; 3) use of audio or visual aids; 4) approach to student participation; 5) apparent range of knowledge; 6) handling of "housekeeping" and clerical chores; 7) reaction to irrelevant interruptions and minor emergencies; 8) rapport with the students; and 9) choice of words. These indicate many things to the evaluator, most importantly, the teacher's application of the principles of learning and knowledge of human behavior.

Evaluation of the change and growth—learning—of students is more difficult. The easiest aspect of the problem is the estimation of the students' factual knowledge. Tests given at the beginning, middle, and conclusion of the course, and later after an interval has elapsed, are likewise fairly easy to assemble and assess. More subtle and difficult to evaluate are the changes in students' attitudes, behavior, and growth that are directly attributable to particular teachers. To this end, rating scales, personality surveys, and attitude inventories have been evolved in lieu of impractical longitudinal or "follow up" studies.

Other popular criteria of teaching effectiveness as discussed by Dressel include:

1. Correlation of measures of student ability and grades;
2. The quality of work in subsequent courses in sequentially organized curricula;
3. Number of students whose choice of majors in a department was directly influenced by a course taken there; and
4. Pre- and post-tests of student growth in course materials.[18]

Dressel suggests that students be questioned about their impressions of the course objectives, experiences, and requirements in terms of scholarly endeavors on their part, intellectual effects upon themselves, and relationships to other courses. Dressel believes this

---

[18] Paul Dressel, "The Current Status of Research on College and University Teaching," in *The Appraisal of Teaching in Large Universities,* a report of a conference supported by the Lilly Endowment, Inc., held at the University of Michigan October 13–14, 1958 (Ann Arbor: University of Michigan Extension Service, 1959), pp. 11–12.

kind of appraisal would be more indicative of teaching effectiveness than student ratings which focus upon the instructor.[19]

Greater emphasis is now being focused upon the college teacher as his own evaluator. This is not unreasonable because the purpose of evaluating teachers is to improve their effectiveness. It follows that any improvement in the quality of instruction must originate with the teacher. The scope and variety of tools employed by college teachers in self-analyses were shown in a study, the results of which are listed below, beginning with the most successful. The ratio of success was computed by dividing the number of successful users by the unsuccessful.

1. Voluntary and continuing colleague discussions or seminars by instructors of a particular course.
2. Comparison check on efficiency using one approach versus efficiency in using another approach.
3. Visit in a colleague's class for purposes of evaluating and improving one's own classes.
4. Planned meetings with colleagues for purposes of evaluating one's own and others' teaching.
5. Systematic search in printed resources for diagnostic tools and procedures for self-evaluation.
6. Yearly written recap of one's own activities and an assessment of the strong and weak aspects of such activities.
7. Action research, a more complex type of field research, for testing both fact and values, utilizing teams of cooperating teachers.
8. Tape or television recording of regular classroom sessions for feedback analysis.
9. Soliciting help of administrators and supervisors in evaluating one's own teaching.
10. Regular luncheons to discuss evaluation of one's own and others' teaching.[20]

Because there are so many variables, besides inexperience and lack of "know-how," which condition the effectiveness of a teacher's performance from year to year, teaching must be continuously evaluated. Factors which can weaken professional vitality are: (a) regarding the doctoral degree as a certificate of perpetual merit

---

[19] Paul L. Dressel, "The Current Status of Research on College and University Teaching," in *The Appraisal of Teaching in Large Universities,* pp. 7–16.

[20] Ray H. Simpson, "Use of Teacher Self-Evaluative Tools for the Improvement of Instruction," American Association of Colleges for Teacher Education *Bulletin,* Vol. XIII, No. 9 (December 30, 1960), p. 4.

obviating the need for further study; (b) diminishing of professional incentives to engage in research; (c) slackening of professional enthusiasm, which can induce bitterness or resignation to being an academic plodder; and (d) changing of one's physical and emotional nature by age, illness, or experience.

Each factor challenges administrators to provide the leadership to create a climate of constant quest. It is a responsibility of the administration to recognize that each faculty member is impelled or deterred by a unique set of circumstances, and to establish procedures to overcome difficulties and improve in-service teachers.

Duties Other Than Instructional

The time spent "on stage" by college teachers is small in relation to the total time demanded by the production. To each classroom experience must be added the time necessary to plan each presentation: prepare the necessary materials, compile appropriate bibliographical references, and pursue the source materials for latest developments in the single discipline or topics under discussion. Also included are meetings with one's own colleagues to discuss their contributions to the field of knowledge, and to weigh one's own competence in terms of the broad spectrum of human knowledge and values.

College teachers set the standards, prepare courses and lectures, advise students, and evaluate their efforts. In addition, the teacher is expected to be available to students who wish a personal conference. Most teachers post regular hours during which they are available in their campus offices. This does not preclude pre-class and post-class meetings, telephone discussions, and appointments outside office hours—all of which are less the exception than the rule. To these student-initiated meetings may be added those initiated by the teacher.

The actual number of hours spent in front of a class may vary from the full professor's six to eight hours weekly to as many as twenty for an instructor. The full professor is usually engaged in research in his remaining time. Administrators are becoming aware that the heavy schedules assigned to instructors can be self-defeating; neophytes, needing more hours of preparation for each hour of class than experienced teachers, are apt to be underprepared.

Dissatisfaction with their performance may discourage, even demoralize, beginners. Unfortunately, time needed for preparation and teaching may preclude their participating in other valuable campus or professional activities, or may prevent completion of their graduate studies.

The average number of classroom hours assigned undergraduate college teachers is about twelve to fifteen weekly. To the minimum twelve, add another twenty-four for preparation (most college teachers expect two hours preparation for each class hour of their students and usually exceed this themselves); three hours of student conferences (a mere half-dozen students can utilize this); three hours for evaluating students' written work (thirty student essays, each of about a thousand words); plus a single two-hour meeting of a professional group. The college teacher, according to this distribution of time, puts in a minimum forty-four hour week. Studies of the actual weekly work load of university faculty members indicate that the average teacher puts in, not just this minimum forty-four hour week, but one greater by 25 per cent or more.

Of the additional responsibilities of college teachers, probably the most pressing is the requirement, common to most four-year institutions, that they pursue some form of research related to their disciplines, and publish the results. It is very nearly impossible to compute the time that is necessary for creativity, but one may be entirely sure that the college teacher must have leisure time in which to think. All highly creative individuals need time—time to dream, to ponder, to explore, and to verify the answer to a problem when its solution seems near, and to test the solution when it emerges.

Countless details consume more time: attendance reports, student records, participation in pre-term registration, chaperoning student social affairs, sponsoring student organizations, responding to research questionnaires, reading and replying to letters from professional organizations, civic groups, parents, salesmen, colleagues, and former students—these do not nearly complete the list.

The college teacher is expected also to participate in intra-institutional and interdepartment committee activities, *ad infinitum*. The American tendency to relegate all major problems to committees extends to academic life. Inevitably a teacher must expect to serve on one or more each semester.

Another activity for college teachers is student counseling, in lieu of, or in conjunction with, the college guidance staff. The college teacher is often asked to address a community group. The rewards vary; the cost is counted in time, since only the most intrepid or experienced dare extemporize.

College teachers also function as educational consultants (to a local committee on secondary school curriculum, for example), as school trustees, and school board members.

Notwithstanding all these demands upon his time, the teacher is expected to be well read, conversant with current issues in the non-academic world, reasonably gregarious, active in public school and civic affairs—and the head of a model American family.

"Publish or Perish" versus Other Alternatives

The university's traditional role as the fountainhead of knowledge has been challenged by a newcomer, the laboratory of industry and technology. Scientists who might once have entered the university's laboratories may now choose among those of expanding industries, which both pay and equip them well. It remains for the university to utilize the research talent at its command to prepare tomorrow's researchers. The university's greatest advantage over the industrial laboratory is its scope and breadth of perspective, and teachers must demonstrate this advantage through their own commitment to research, whatever their disciplines.

The persistent emphasis upon published research as *the* criterion for professional advancement in institutions of higher education has been a double-edged blade. While it has stimulated many faculty members to attack the unknown independently and to produce significant and valuable learnings, it has caused others to waste time and effort in the production of what one writer terms "minutiae and trivia."

The difference lies probably in the climate of the institution. Worthwhile teaching and research demand an institutional climate directed toward the goal of service, and concerned primarily with what Van Doren terms the "essential things: the essential questions, rather than the essential answers."[21]

---

[21] Mark Van Doren, "Teacher and Student in the Search for Truth," *College Teaching as a Career* (Washington: American Council on Education, Committee on College Teaching, 1961), p. 8.

Research within an institution is encouraged by:

1. time provided in the administrative estimation of the individual's total assignment for reading, thinking and assimilating, as well as for experimental research. Instructional loads may occupy a quarter to a half of the professor's time, the rest being devoted to research;
2. resources in the form of financial support, equipment, facilities, materials, and clerical and secretarial assistance, as well as the services of specialists in design, statistics, computer programming, etc.;
3. interdepartmental assistance and consultive services, available because such time allocations have been provided by the administration;
4. communication between members of various disciplines, made possible through provisions for attendance and participation in state, regional, and national deliberations;
5. opportunity, encouragement, and support by the entire staff, faculty, and administrators of the institution to promising research talent.[22]

Perhaps the most telling form of encouragement is the institution's willingness to allow the individual to pursue "his own interest, at his own pace, and in his own way."[23]

Institutional Leadership

Whether he be president, dean, or department chairman, the administrator must exert, maintain, and develop leadership. He must himself exert professional leadership in defining and fulfilling the purposes of his institution; he must maintain (and expand) the leadership of the institution in its particular areas of excellence; and he must develop the leadership potential of his staff members.

There are general qualifications, peculiarly conducive to educational leadership, which must be possessed by the administrator and sought by the faculty. A leader must possess a personal philosophy of education which he has clearly defined and to which he is firmly committed. He must be fully aware of the purposes, potentialities, and limitations of his institution. He must have a little

---

[22] Committee on Studies Report, "Research and Study in Education," American Association of Colleges for Teacher Education *Bulletin*, Egon G. Guba (ed.), Vol. XIV, No. 11 (December 1961).

The foregoing statement of principles and institutional practices in its original, complete form was developed to assist administrators implement research.
[23] *Ibid.*

of the actor's histrionic appeal. He must combine a critical, analytical mind with an intense humanity.

The primary element conditioning leadership activities in a faculty is the possession of these qualities by the administrators. Some of the conditions which usually obtain when this element is present are:

1. that responsibility and authority are delegated to appropriate personnel in accordance with the problem to be resolved;
2. that faculty participation in the formulation and solution of institutional problems which are genuinely and obviously significant is encouraged, and rewarded with the satisfaction of seeing these recommendations implemented;
3. that a climate of mutual respect assures even the holders of minority opinions of an attentive audience.

Obviously, the quality of its educational leadership is the key to the total atmosphere of an institution, upon which hinges the extent and value of its experimentation and research, the nature and scope of its professional activities, its over-all rating as a great institution, and the amount of leadership within its faculty.

Improved Working Conditions

Institutions of higher education are experiencing the greatest building boom in their history. To accommodate the incoming hordes of students, old buildings are being refurbished and new ones are being erected, some hastily and inadequately conceived, others well planned and functional.

Ways are now being developed whereby a faculty will be able to extend its instructional potential far beyond the statistical limitations of normal pupil-teacher ratios. University laboratories contain instruments undreamed of only a few years ago, new purposes for which may be ascertained tomorrow. No aspect of the institutional plant is so minute as to escape attention, study, and improvement. Television, tapes, transparencies, films, recordings, teaching machines, language laboratories and promising innovational media are common equipment. Educational Facilities Laboratories estimates that more than 130 million dollars will be spent during the 1960's on language laboratories alone.[25] There has been an up-

---

[25] Educational Facilities Laboratories, *Here They Learn: First Annual Report* (New York: Educational Facilities Laboratories, Ford Foundation, 1959), p. 20.

surge in the number of traveling exhibits available for instructional purposes, ranging from artifacts to zoological specimens. To produce esthetically enchanting buildings with appropriately landscaped grounds, some of the nation's most capable architects have been employed.

Depending upon where they are employed, all this means either a great deal or very little to college teachers. So tremendous has been the financial drain of putting existing college buildings into serviceable condition and maintaining them, that the building of new facilities has been minimal at some institutions.

Often student populations have outstripped both the projections and the accommodations. As a consequence, many teachers are attempting to cope with over-sized classes in under-sized rooms. Their more fortunate colleagues may be facing large classes also, but in rooms designed and built to accommodate them. Reflecting the emphasis on large group presentations and small working units and discussions, new buildings feature sliding walls and hexagonal rooms for necessary flexibility, perceptual experience, and demonstrations of various kinds.

In modern structures specific space allocations are being assigned for staff offices. Faculty members find the privacy afforded by these rooms of great psychological value in their student counseling conferences, and in their own personal study, writing, and research.

The endless flood of forms, statements, reports, and other data-gathering instruments which deluge college teachers has not substantially diminished, but faculty members' relief from the laborious task of responding to these inquiries is imminent because of modern electronic computers and business machines.

Faculty clubs, where staff members may obtain meals and the company of colleagues, are among the conveniences instituted, along with adequate reserved parking facilities for the many teachers, who commute from within a radius of a hundred miles.

These examples of pleasant changes in the working conditions of college teachers do not, of themselves, guarantee the ability to retain top faculty members of an institution. Working conditions, as has been demonstrated throughout this chapter, encompass a multitude of factors.

Administrators are becoming increasingly attentive toward the less physical, more professional aspects of working conditions. Their efforts are more aptly reflected in obtaining adequate salary schedules, adjustment of teaching loads on the basis of other professional activities, reduction of committee assignments, grants-in-aid, salaried sabbaticals for worthy enterprises of reliable staff members, and public recognition for meritorious teaching service.

The working conditions of college teachers—physical, financial, and professional—are improving, and promise to continue to do so at an accelerated pace for the foreseeable future.

CHAPTER VI

Trends and Prospects

The trends and experiments that will be described in the remaining pages constitute some, although not all, of the efforts directed toward staffing colleges and universities of the United States with more and better teachers.

Early Identification of Talent

The problems of expanding demand for college attendance are being attacked on several fronts in institutions of higher education across the land. Admissions standards, for example, are being raised, tending to favor the bright students who decide early upon their academic goals and work toward them. Acceleration is becoming a widely accepted procedure. Talented youths are given enriched programs at the elementary level and college-level subject matter in secondary school, and are admitted to college with advanced standing—all with the announced purpose of allowing capable students to complete their undergraduate, professional, and special education at earlier than normal ages, thereby enabling them to spend more time in their professions.

In such circumstances, it is inevitable that colleges and universities begin to look to the undergraduate population as a source of future college teachers. Through processes of early identification and personal influence, professors are attempting to introduce undergraduates of scholarly promise to a teaching field by permitting them to serve as teaching or laboratory assistants. Many educators are echoing Carmichael's suggestion[1] that college teachers be recruited in the junior year of the undergraduate school, making it quite likely that a study such as Stecklein and Eckert's in 1958,[2]

---

[1] Oliver C. Carmichael, *Graduate Education: A Critique and a Program* (New York: Harper & Row, Publishers, Inc., 1961), p. 125.

[2] John E. Stecklein and Ruth E. Eckert, *An Exploratory Study of Factors Influencing the Choice of College Teaching as a Career,* A Final Report, Cooperative Research Project, U.S. Office of Education (Minneapolis: University of Minnesota, Bureau of Institutional Research, January 1948), p. 40.

if conducted a decade later, would report considerable alteration in the "time of decision" category. The 1958 study showed that the majority of college teachers decided to enter the field late— *after* receiving their first degree, many of them during or after graduate school.

Guidance and Counseling

About half the respondents in Stecklein and Eckert's study mentioned counseling by administrators, guidance personnel, and college teachers as being influential in their selection of college teaching as a career.[3] This trend does not appear to have diminished. It might be said that college teaching in the United States has reached a mid-point in its transition from a profession into which teachers have drifted, to one like medicine, where the future practitioners are being actively identified, nurtured, recruited, and prepared for career service. From this point, the important problems facing college teaching will demand expertness in guidance and not just mere frequency in counseling.

It is now generally accepted that academically outstanding students in any subject discipline are potential faculty material. Through the efforts of national professional organizations, representing the several fields of specialization, leaders in the field of higher education, institutional administrators, and state legislators, the responsibility for encouraging capable students to seek careers in college teaching has been placed upon present college teachers and department heads, as well as upon guidance personnel. But no authority has been clearly delegated the formidable task of supplying an adequate number of college teachers for the period directly ahead. Currently, it seems to be everyone's responsibility but no-one's obligation. This matter surely deserves more attention in every faculty.

Support through Scholarships and Fellowships

In 1962 the House Advisory Group on Higher Education, in its final report to the House Committee on Education and Labor, made, among others, the following recommendations:

---

[3] *Ibid.*, p. 41.

... that provision be made under NDEA for a program (similar to the present NSF science faculty program) of institutes, faculty fellowships, and visiting professorships to increase the effectiveness of college teachers in all fields; and that matching grants be provided to institutions of higher education for support of similar faculty development programs under institutional auspices.[4]

These recommendations reflect the widespread national concern with the problem of financing higher education appropriately and adequately, as well as with that of providing enough competent faculty for colleges and universities. Thanks to this growing concern, millions of dollars are being contributed annually to higher education by private foundations, corporations, interested citizens, and the federal government. Grants have done such an enormous amount of good in supporting research, providing building facilities and libraries, and expanding scholarships, fellowships, awards, and aid, that the average layman may wonder why the financial problems of higher education seem to persist unabated.

Perhaps the reason lies in the control exercised by donors. Each benefactor contributes to the purpose, institution, school, and department of his choice. While this in no way diminishes the value of the contribution in terms of the recipient, it does tend to produce an over-all patchiness in higher education. Certain disciplines clearly identifiable with the national interest are favored in times of international tension, while others languish for want of support. The sciences, for example, have received amazing financial aid under the direct stimulus of Russian space achievements, while the humanities literally have gone begging. More importantly, high prestige schools appear to receive the lion's share of support, which enables them to grow in strength with high quality personnel and students, while impoverished but well intentioned institutions must make do with whatever the king of the beasts leaves. Clearly, small progress toward over-all excellence may be expected until a much more reasonable and equitable program of support is devised.

Meanwhile some college teachers are recipients of scholarships, fellowships, awards, and grants to support their graduate studies, their in-service professional enrichment, and their researches. In

---

[4] U.S. Department of Health, Education, and Welfare, Office of Education, Higher Education Division, *Higher Education*, Vol. XVIII, No. 5 (Washington: Government Printing Office, March 1962), p. 18.

many institutions a staff member is designated to keep well abreast of available scholarships and fellowships, so that he may disseminate such information to students and faculty colleagues. Astute faculty members, especially newcomers, become well-acquainted with him.

Professional Preparation and Supervised Teaching

The criticism of college teaching *per se,* that appears in an earlier chapter, focuses the attention of those concerned with higher education, especially those in administrative positions, upon the persistent problem of preparing college teachers to teach. Many still believe, despite research outcomes to the contrary, that the expert in a subject field is automatically an expert teacher, and that courses in teaching are a minor, almost incidental, or even an unnecessary provision.

Another group of scholars, similar to the first, admit that some pedagogical features are involved in the teaching of various subjects, since the behavorial sciences have confirmed principles which can be applied to teaching. But these scholars believe that each discipline is so unique that the supervision and instruction of prospective college teachers should be left solely to their subject major departments, eliminating the possible contributions of professional schools or departments of education.

Again, there are groups of scholars who would permit cooperative action, since they believe that students are better teachers if they receive their preparation in how to teach from the professional schools of education and their subject matter content from the appropriate subject matter department. This latter viewpoint, calling for a close integration of the two programs, presupposes two conditions: (1) communication between the subject matter and instructional specialists; and (2) joint supervision of all students' initial teaching experiences.

The foregoing viewpoints represent three divergent steps of development in contemporary thought related to the preparation of college teachers. As in every other area in American education, all possible shades of opinion and practice may be found operating in collegiate institutions. Thus, Axelrod found: (1) graduate students at Vanderbilt University being "loaned" to other institutions to teach under their supervision after a course in teaching methodology; (2) a graduate minor in college and university teaching being offered at Oregon State University in which the departments of the graduate school are responsible for preparing students to teach and for providing them with opportunities to gain experience as laboratory assistants or as teaching assistants; and (3) an eclectic philosophy operative at Tulane University, where each department undertakes in its own way to prepare its own Ph.D. students to teach. One department holds seminars for student discussions; another assigns books to be read, reported upon, and discussed; and yet another, gives a course in the history of education followed by a two-semester period of supervised teaching. During the first semester, students must attend, teach occasionally and grade papers; during the second, the student is assigned the full responsibility for one section of the course.[5]

To argue in support of a systematic approach to college teacher preparation is in no way to derogate the place and importance of liberal studies. Teaching skill without substance in content is as ridiculous to consider as is the idea that the Ph.D. degree is a guarantee of teaching proficiency, automatically conferring the role of master teacher upon the recipient.

Whether the mastery of liberal studies, a discipline, and research skills is sufficient to insure success in college teaching, or whether knowledge of learning theory and demonstrable skill in teaching are likewise essential, has been a long and at times bitter debate.

An inherent falseness becomes increasingly noticeable in the alleged dichotomy between the two positions and in the implication that these are mutually exclusive:

> . . . as a group, the teachers of [both] professional education [and] liberal arts strongly favor including a sizeable portion of nonprofessional subject matter in all undergraduate curricula.[6]

The study from which this quotation is taken shows concern with the liberal studies component in several undergraduate professional curriculums of which teacher education is only one. It

---

[5] Joseph Axelrod (ed.), *Graduate Study for Future College Teachers* (Washington: American Council on Education, 1959), pp. 23–29.

[6] Paul L. Dressel and Margaret F. Lorimer, *The Attitudes of Liberal Arts Faculties Toward Liberal and Professional Education* (New York: Institution of Higher Education, Teachers College, Columbia University, 1960), p. vi.

is concerned also with the attitudes of professors in professional schools toward the liberal arts; with the attitudes of professors in liberal arts college toward both liberal and professional studies; and with the place of the graduate school in relation to undergraduate humanities and teacher preparing programs.

The divergent views held by the respondents in this study reveals that in liberal arts colleges there is a large segment of the total sampling which is seriously at odds with their own colleagues in their estimation of the value of professional education and their definition of liberal education. This group also includes those who equate the liberal arts with any narrow discipline in which a student can "prove" his intellect. These respondents are of the opinion that the ends of professional education are best served merely by an apprenticeship after graduation.

The attitudes of faculty personnel in professional schools moreover shows there is conflict among themselves about programs in liberal studies. For example, there are those who hold that any course is liberal if it broadens a student's perception or deepens his humanitarian interest.[7]

The widely divergent views and attitudes reported in this study indicate that there is necessarily a vast amount of ground work to be worked out before the humanities and professional education professors can work together harmoniously. The respondents seem to regard the "ideal" undergraduate curriculum as one devoting from 36 to 50 per cent of the hours to breadth of subject matter, 26 to 35 per cent to depth in one's major subject field, and 11 to 25 per cent to professional courses.[8]

Clearly, the problem is no longer whether general education, liberal studies, and professional courses are necessary, but in what proportions relative to each other they best fulfill their functions. New approaches to the preparation of college teachers mark this well as they merge academic and professional efforts in a way unthought a decade ago.

Some multi-purpose institutions, for example, are utilizing the dynamics of diversity to develop newer programs which reflect the thinking of both the graduate and professional school faculties. Through the cooperative planning of representatives of both fac-

---

[7] *Ibid.*, p. 37.
[8] *Ibid.*, p. 30.

ulties, a university is able to give students an appreciation of what makes for teacher effectiveness and a sequential set of experiences in courses that reveal the multi-dimensional quality of the task of teaching. Frequently, this is accomplished through a series of graduate seminars intended to examine contemporary educational theory and practice, to apply psychological principles to the teaching of subject matter, to use evaluative processes in the determination of effective classroom instruction, and to employ specific instructional skills, methods, and materials.

The formulation of recruitment criteria, curricular requirements, and content for college teacher preparation programs clearly cannot be a unilateral effort by any one department. It must require the combined efforts of all the academic disciplines, if for no other reason than that the college teachers whom they will produce must serve all the disciplines. This challenge may eventually unite university faculties of various disciplines into a more cohesive body, to the everlasting relief of subsequent generations of students.

Much valuable time has been lost, and many words wasted in purposeless accusations and counter-accusations by members of the various disciplines concerning ways to prepare better teachers; but the tensions inherent in the problem are finally subsiding and it now appears that faculty members are beginning to face up to the question cooperatively in the spirit of joint enterprise.

Internships

A promising addition to the preparatory programs for college teachers is the internship—an amalgam of supervised teaching and medical intern-type programs—being instituted at Yale University, Syracuse University, the University of Rochester, and several other universities. Such programs have several advantages over the widely used practice of assistantships. For one, the internship program as a training ground for good teaching is an integral part of a graduate student's program rather than a burdensome responsibility appended to it. For another, internship implies a period of training, rather than a testing period, where students' errors are diagnosed so their performance can be improved, rather than compared with the performance of experienced practitioners. In addition, internship programs actively involve the entire preparing faculty as a group with the intern. This eliminates the danger where a single supervising teacher is assigned, that he will be selected more because of his availability than because of his superior knowledge and skill in teaching. When availability is the criterion, mediocrity is often compounded.

Which preparatory pattern will eventually take precedence will probably depend upon factors such as how widely publicized the philosophy, procedures, criteria of success, evaluation and outcomes of today's infant programs become. It will also depend on how objective the graduates of those programs—tomorrow's college teachers—will be in analyzing and assessing the values and/or handicaps to themselves that are directly attributable to the programs which prepared them.

Placement Service

Placement service is becoming increasingly an institutional responsibility in American higher education. It is not, however, a responsibility in the sense of "selling" one's graduates to other institutions in order to build a placement record that will attract prospective students. One of the happier circumstances accompanying the shortage of qualified college teachers has been the alteration of this focus. The function of the placement service is less to provide the graduate or degree recipient with a position, and more to provide the opportunity for a mutually advantageous relationship between the prospective college teacher and the hiring institution.

To this end, changes have been taking place within the structure of the placement service. Estimating the probability of a happy mating between prospective teacher and institution demands a great deal of knowledge of both. Hence, placement officers, to be fully effective, need dossiers to reveal as much as possible about the candidates, as persons, and their academic, social, and extracurricular history.

Alert placement officers also build files on each of the institutions that are prospective employers. These files usually are cumulative and contain whatever pertinent information is available. Basic information generally consists of an institution's stated purposes and objectives, printed materials on specific faculty beliefs or assumptions, documents on faculty personnel policies, organization, and salary schedules, catalogues listing curricular offerings that are designed to achieve the avowed institutional goals, literature to reflect conditions of faculty service likely to promote high morale, and information concerning legal and voluntary accreditation, if any. Where possible, the placement officer tries diligently to provide his registrants with objective information about such areas as the prevailing faculty climate, attitudes, biases, prejudices, mores, and the nature of the faculty-administrator relationships. Such aspects of an institution, though critically important, are seldom overt, and are available only to placement officers who by experience are good listeners and consummate diplomats, and are well acquainted with many sources of information.

Where well informed, well staffed placement services are maintained, an employing institution with strong research orientation is unlikely to find its newly recruited teacher an indifferent researcher, and a college with a militantly religious faculty is unlikely to find an agnostic among those recommended to it as prospective appointees.

Graduate Housing

Since graduate students frequently attend schools at institutions other than those in which they acquired their baccalaureate degrees, they are often "unknown quantities" to their new professors and advisers. If these graduate students are married and have established homes in communities remote from the campus, they are present only for classes, library work, or conference attendance, and tend to remain unknown quantities. The larger the classes in which these graduate students are, and the less inclined toward loquacity they may be, the more nearly total is their anonymity.

Advising such students is a risky undertaking; their difficulties are often undetected until they either "flounder" or drop out of graduate school. Assessing them in terms of successful placement becomes largely guesswork: the cultural and social advantages which the institution may offer may have been lost upon them and, due to the time-honored custom of professors to award "safe" C's or B's to those students whose faces and names they have difficulty in associating because of numbers, the graduate work such students do can be evaluated only with difficulty.

Realizing this, colleges and universities attempt to keep seminars small, to encourage the graduate student to be an on-campus resident, and to bring to the graduate program some of the important characteristics of the undergraduate years—those that are peripheral to the class, library, and conference nucleus. Graduate residence centers have been established on most university campuses, offering students a wide range of interpersonal, social, and cultural activities. The centers offer a place for informal student-faculty contacts, and for listening to records or discussing new concepts with fellow classmates. They also provide a forum where elected representatives of the graduate student body may keep the institution's top administrators aware of student thought. While these centers have attracted many of the unmarried graduate students, their utilization by married students, whose time is taken up with family and occupational responsibilities, has been limited.

One specification, operative at most graduate schools, that candidates for the doctor's degree must spend at least one full year "in residence" has frequently done little good, and merely imposes on the often already overburdened married students the necessity for commuting and for preparing for twice the usual number of courses in a given semester. Regional accreditation standards have led institutions to encourage, if not demand, doctoral students to take the "in residence" requirement quite literally. Failure to comply usually results in a student's being dropped.

To spend a semester or more on campus, graduate students must have time: summers, sabbaticals, and leaves of absence are utilized. They must have money: grants in-aid, scholarships, loans, and stipends for families are arranged with the institution. When available, personal earnings or carefully hoarded family savings are often tapped. Graduate students must have living quarters: off-campus facilities with private citizens are inspected and approved, and on-campus facilities are refurbished, refurnished, or occasionally new quarters are built. And, frequently, undergraduate dormitories are utilized during summer vacations. Probably the specially designed graduate housing facility and the utilization of undergraduate dormitories in summer sessions are the means of greatest potential, especially in view of the pronounced trend toward all-year (three semester and four quarter) utilization of institutional facilities.

Not all institutions can adopt the Harvard House Plan, but each college can find ways whereby housing can contribute to the intellectual maturation of students.

As the number of graduate students continues to increase, apartment buildings are looming side-by-side with student dormitories, affording married graduate students the advantage of on-campus residence, and the institutions a potential reservoir of teaching interns and assistants-in-residence. If housing and eating facilities are also expected to contribute to the cultural climate of the campus, they must obviously be the responsibility of the director of student life or dean of instruction—not the responsibility of the department of buildings and grounds or the business office.

Participation in Problems Related to Instruction

In its journal, the American Association of University Professors issued a statement of principles concerning faculty participation in college and university government. This statement indicated that faculty members are entitled to much, and in some areas primary, responsibility for determining educational policies involving subject matter, instructional methods, research support, academic performance, granting of degrees, student regulations, academic calendars, new schools and divisions, community services, faculty appointments, reappointment and tenure, selection of administrative officers and department heads, and budget allocations and expenditures.[9] There are few institutions which cannot boast of instances wherein their faculties have admirably demonstrated such competency in one or another of the areas listed.

Stimulation and Support of Institutional Studies

Sooner or later every institution of higher education must take a long, hard look at its own operations. The basic purpose is to improve the institution's total effectiveness and to determine whether its operations are attaining the ends for which they were established. Subsidiary reasons might include preparing a plan for the measurement of outcomes for evaluating teams from accredit-

---

[9] "Faculty Participation in College and University Government," AAUP *Bulletin*, Vol. XLVIII, No. 4 (December 1962), 321–23.

ing associations, estimating the need and feasibility of new curricular programs, measuring the effectiveness of the library, locating sources of symptomatic disturbances among students, faculty, or staff, and eradicating impediments to organizational efficiency. For such evaluation the office of institutional research is conceived.

There are as many kinds of knowledge necessary to the successful operation of institutional research offices as there are services in institutions of higher education. Does a particular schedule of instruction contribute to the fullest utilization of space? Are the procedures employed in the bookkeeping department efficient? Are the food services being fully utilized by the student body, and if not, why not? Are the admissions procedures operating in the best interests of all the candidates, as well as of the institution? Should the new dormitories accommodate more than two students per room? How have the graduates of 19— fared professionally as a result of their college experiences? The possibilities for research to support decisions in the many large and small problems which daily confront college and university personnel are infinite.

Realizing that such research necessitates some sort of organized attack, universities have established offices of institutional research to coordinate, facilitate, launch, and otherwise implement it. The personnel of such offices are specialists both in research techniques and in the major areas of institutional organization and function. Computers of various descriptions, having justified their initial expense in savings of time, manpower, and money, have become integral parts of institutional research operations. When graduate students are afforded opportunities to participate in the work of these offices, their appreciation of the complexity of institutions of higher education is assured. An additional benefit accrues in their subsequent sensitivity to institutional problems and competence in contributing to their solution. Such an experience is a likely candidate for inclusion in future preparatory programs for college teachers.

Salary and Welfare Provisions

Ivory towers notwithstanding, college teachers must provide themselves and their families with the substantial shelter of financial security. This implies adequate salaries, reasonable assurance of continued employment, sufficient insurance to cover costs of illness, and appropriate retirement incomes, in approximately that order of importance.

Heim and Baumol report the outcomes of a compensation survey conducted for 1961–1962 by the AAUP.[10] The fringe benefits most commonly reported were contributions by institutions to retirement funds, Social Security, group life insurance, medical protection, permanent disability insurance, housing, and tuition for faculty children. The authors make the point that institutional funds for faculty compensation are relatively fixed; therefore, there are some disadvantages to the alleged "benefits," since they involve a proportionate decrease in actual salary, and, unless determined on an individual basis, may force individuals to accept benefits they do not want. The average institution was found to pay about eight per cent of a faculty salary in countable benefits. Interestingly enough, the private institutions surveyed far outstripped their public counterparts in almost all the benefit programs. Modest as these beginnings may be, they point toward the assumption of welfare responsibility for their personnel by institutions of higher education.

The uninitiated will find in the back issues of the AAUP *Bulletin* a history of that organization's continuing struggle to establish and maintain the "job security" of college teachers. The entire profession has reaped the benefits of its searching, impartial investigations of cases wherein abridgement of academic rights or freedom has been suspected. So much respect has the organization engendered that its statements of policy exert significant influence on the nation's colleges and universities. One of the most recent statements advocates a year's terminal appointment in all cases of dismissal not involving moral turpitude. A reaction to this idea is eagerly anticipated.

With monetary inflation, increased longevity, and a relatively high standard of living, college teachers are quite likely to find themselves at a financial disadvantage upon retirement. Heim and Baumol report that most individuals who enter a retirement plan at age 35 and stay to retire at age 68 can expect the incomes of

---

[10] Peggy Heim and William J. Baumol, "On the Fringe: The State of Retirement Contributions and Other Non-Pecuniary Faculty Benefits," AAUP *Bulletin,* Vol. XLVIII, No. 4 (December 1962), 346–58.

their final active years to be approximately halved upon retirement.[11] Such circumstances have prompted more than a few professors emeriti to seek further employment, and have led many institutions to supplement the income of those left in dire straits. Prudent professors have long recognized the advantages of savings accounts and sound investments, but their salaries often have precluded this, especially when there were many dependents.

The Mills Bill, which proposed diverting part of professorial salaries to a retirement program and the income taxes on that part to the purchase of annuity benefits, marked an increasing legislative interest in the problem. But, as Heim and Baumol conclude, the final solution reverts to the old theme—higher academic salaries.[12]

Adequate Research Library

To facilitate a 1957–58 self-study, the Columbia University Libraries suggested five levels of completeness as evaluative criteria for the library of a university:

1. *Basic information collections,* comprised of minimal resources for subjects outside the scope of present instruction;
2. *Working collections,* comprised of subject holdings in the broad outlines and main historical outlines, but reflecting accurately the needs of the institution as defined by its undergraduate courses of study;
3. *General research collections,* comprised of accessions adequate for graduate students and including the major portion of materials required for dissertations and independent research;
4. *Comprehensive collections,* comprised of materials which expand the graduate research collection to include a wider selection of holdings for current and historical research, in all pertinent languages or translations, plus documentary and original source material; and
5. *Exhaustive collections,* comprised of everything written on given subjects in all languages, editions, and translations.

Building library collections suitable to the purposes of a university involves tremendous sums of money plus the efforts of three categories of people: (1) *selectors*—librarians and faculty members knowledgeable enough can anticipate needs and select acqui-

---

[11] *Ibid.,* p. 353.
[12] *Ibid.,* p. 356.

sitions discriminately; they should be possessed of both language and subject competency; (2) *contributors*—since many of the best collections are owned by private citizens, institutions which desire such holdings should earnestly endeavor to obtain them as gifts, or, failing this, obtain options to buy. Here persuasive faculty members or administrators often perform their most memorable services to their institutions.[13] Foundation gifts to support libraries, such as those of the Louis Calder Foundation to Kalamazoo College ($100,000) and the Kresge Foundation to Notre Dame ($100,-000) benefit the entire institution and often make the difference between collections which fall into the first two or into the last three of Columbia's categories; (3) *maintainers*—this group includes primarily the librarians, but also all those who use its facilities, especially those using research materials which are fragile and irreplaceable. Lest faculty members underestimate the importance of the librarians, many institutions, Harvard for example, give them professorial rank.

One of the first targets of accreditation evaluating teams is an institution's library, for it is truly said that the quality of a university's program seldom exceeds that of its library—the heart of the institution.

Implications for Future Programs

It is impossible to think of higher education and the responsibilities which the space age and the population explosion have imposed upon it except in terms of adjustment, flexibility, and redirection. Since technological development accelerates social and educational change, it may be assumed that creative ideas and new and high quality approaches to preparing college teachers will come into vogue.

More than ever before, the task ahead will require team effort of a high order. The intense interest in education, on the part of the academic fraternity as well as of the public, may help to spur the next phase of development—a dramatically new way to prepare college teachers in large numbers. To do so, will require each graduate school to face realistically the task of devising adequate

---

[13] Maurice F. Tauber, "The Faculty and the Development of Library Collections," *Journal of Higher Education*, Vol. XXXII, No. 8 (November 1961), 454–55.

and practical plans for overcoming faculty inertia and of unlocking the shackles of traditionalism in curriculum patterns.

It is to be expected that the changes will be revolutionary in character rather than mere adaptations of threadbare practices. They will need to be tried and proved before they replace cherished premises. New subject matter arrangements and new curricula will be a cause of concern to all who prefer conventional patterns. But that evolution is most fruitful which involves changes in students, in courses, and in the entire program.

How then will preparatory programs for the future take shape? Will they continue to emphasize for each future college teacher his responsibility for inspired teaching, or for systematic research, or for graduate training slanted heavily toward scholarly writing— or possibly all three? Will the plans for college teacher preparation combine through joint programs the best efforts of the faculties of the graduate schools and of the professional schools of education? Or will the programs be administered solely by the graduate schools, with the responsibility for developing the ability to teach assigned to the several subject major departments? One wonders, too, whether graduate curricula will become increasingly specialized or more broadly interdisciplinary. In either case, to what degree will the graduate school faculties be concerned: (a) with the purposes of instruction; (b) with the teacher's role of imparting a love of learning, a respect for academic excellence, and an awareness of the joys that accrue to one who works with human materials; (c) with the length of time it takes the average candidate to acquire a doctor's degree; (d) with the quality of programs as well as with omitted subject areas; and (e) with student-faculty relationships that are conducive to open communication?

If the trends which are now apparent in American higher education fulfill their promise, the coming decades should find college teaching enjoying unequivocal professional status. College teachers will probably choose their profession, complete their graduate education, and begin teaching at an earlier age than is now customary. The doctoral degree is unlikely to lose its status as the profession's hallmark of distinction and its holders undoubtedly will increase both numerically and proportionately; but growing criticism of traditional research-oriented Ph.D. programs will result in changes for those who plan to teach.

With further breakthroughs in research in the behavioral sciences, professional education, guidance, and evaluation will have a greater role in the preparation of college teachers than is now the case. The support of higher education will be seen more and more as a public responsibility when the vast numbers of parents of lower and middle class socio-economic status who now plan college educations for their offspring begin to encounter the financial facts of life. The support has quite properly shifted in the direction of increased federal aid.

It now appears that internships and on-campus residence will become firmly entrenched in the preparation patterns for college teachers. Graduate schools probably will face up to the Foreign-language requirements as specified by the department in which a student selects his field of concentration by offering non-credit, free evening courses, with formal instruction of a mature and efficient caliber.

Teachers will contribute more and more fully in areas now considered to be solely the administrative province or the role of the trustees. Their interdisciplinary and interinstitutional activities will increase, dispelling old animosities. Even the dichotomy between what-to-teach and how-to-teach may be relegated to mythology. But the emphasis on research and publication by university faculty members promises to continue.

Will these predictions of change actually materialize? The incoming generation of college teachers will provide the answer. Trends which currently appear to be rising or cresting are the product of yesteryear's professional educators. The beginning college teachers whom they have prepared will reflect their teaching. Some of the new college teachers will be almost indistinguishable from their own professors in their attitudes, opinions, and even, perhaps, in their mannerisms. Others may be completely and deliberately the antithesis of those who prepared them. Those whose professors taught them best will reflect only their habits of objective, analytical, deeply contemplative thought. They will formulate, as they were taught, their own commitments, and then support and defend them.

If the reader begins to note a certain circular tendency in this train of thought, he is quite correct. Tomorrow's faculty will contain its normal proportions of conservatives, liberals, and radicals, fairly similar to today's. The issues which will unite them to determine the future's "trends" are unforeseeable. Perhaps time will demonstrate that techniques already exist to improve markedly all phases of classroom teaching, and that feasible plans can be instituted on any campus for the improvement of educational effectiveness.

Bibliography

Baskin, Samuel, ed., *Higher Education: Some Newer Developments.* New York: McGraw-Hill Book Company, 1965.

Berelson, Bernard, *Graduate Education in the United States.* New York: McGraw-Hill Book Company, 1960.

Brickman, William W., and Stanely Lehrer, eds., *A Century of Higher Education: Classical Citadel to Collegiate Colossus.* New York: Society for the Advancement of Education, 1962.

Brubacher, John S., and Willis Rudy, *Higher Education in Transition, An American History: 1636–1956.* New York: Harper & Row, Publishers, Inc., 1958.

Carmichael, Oliver C., *Graduate Education: A Critique and a Program.* New York: Harper & Row, Publishers, Inc., 1961.

Dressel, Paul L., *et al., Evaluation in Higher Education.* Boston: Houghton Mifflin Company, 1961.

Gardner, John W., *et al., The Pursuit of Excellence: Education and the Future of America.* Panel Report V of the Special Studies Project, Rockefeller Brothers Fund. New York: Doubleday & Company, Inc., 1958.

Henderson, Algo D., *Policies and Practices in Higher Education.* New York: Harper & Row, Publishers, Inc., 1960.

Hofstadter, Richard, and Wilson Smith, eds., *American Higher Education: A Documentary History.* Chicago: University of Chicago Press, 1961. Two volumes.

Mushkin, Selma J., ed., *Economics of Higher Education.* U.S. Department of Health, Education, and Welfare, Office of Education, Bulletin 1962, No. 5 OE–50027, Washington; U.S. Government Printing Office, 1962.

National Education Association, Research Division. *Salaries Paid and Salary Practices in Universities, Colleges, and Junior Colleges, 1963–64.* Higher Education Series. Research Report 1964–R3. Washington, D.C.: National Education Association, February 1964.

National Education Association, Research Division. *Teacher Supply and Demand in Universities, Colleges, and Junior Colleges, 1961–62.* Research Report 1963-R3. Higher Education Series. Washington, D.C.: the Association, May 1963.

McKeachie, Wilbert, and Gregory A. Kimble, *Teaching Tips: A Guidebook for the Beginning College Teacher* (4th ed.). Ann Arbor, Michigan: G. Wahr Publishing Co., 1960.

McGlothin, William J., *Patterns of Professional Education.* New York: G. P. Putnam's Sons, 1960.

McGrath, Earl J., *Liberal Education in the Professions*. New York: Institute of Higher Education, Teachers College, Columbia University Press, 1959.

Medsker, Leland L., *The Junior College: Progress and Prospect*. New York: McGraw-Hill Book Company, 1960.

Peterson, Houston, ed., *Great Teachers: Portrayed by Those Who Studied Under Them*. New Brunswick, N.J.: Rutgers University Press, 1946.

Sanford, Nevitt, ed., *The American College*. New York: John Wiley & Sons, Inc., 1962.

Schmidt, George P., *The Liberal Arts College: A Chapter in American Cultural History*. New Brunswick, N.J.: Rutgers University Press, 1957.

Umstattd, J. G., *College Teaching: Background, Theory and Practice*. Washington, D.C.: The University Press, 1964.

Wilson, Logan, ed., *Emerging Patterns in American Higher Education*. Washington: American Council on Education, 1965.

Index

115